DORDOGNE
gastronomique

DORDOGNE
gastronomique

VICKY JONES

FOREWORD BY ANNE WILLAN

PHOTOGRAPHY BY HAMISH PARK

SERIES EDITOR MARIE-PIERRE MOINE

ABBEVILLE PRESS PUBLISHERS

NEW YORK   LONDON   PARIS

First published in the United States
of America in 1994 by
Abbeville Press
488 Madison Avenue
New York NY 10022

First published in Great Britain in 1994 by
Conran Octopus Limited
37 Shelton Street
London WC2H 9HN

ISBN 1-55859-873-1

Senior Editor **SARAH PEARCE**
Art Editor **KAREN BOWEN**
Text Editor **CLAIRE CALMAN**
Editorial Assistant **CHARLOTTE COLEMAN-SMITH**
Production **JILL MACEY**

NOTES ON RECIPES Both metric and imperial quantities
are given. Use either all metric or all imperial, as the
two are not interchangeable.

CONTENTS

FOREWORD

The fame of Dordogne cooking owes much to the resourcefulness of its cooks. With the exception of a few river valleys and the plains fringing the Atlantic, this is not a fertile region; rocky uplands predominate, slashed by rivers like the Dordogne. On this unpromising terrain are produced some of France's gastronomic masterpieces, notably truffles – which must still be rootled out by a sow or dog trained to the business – and fattened geese and ducks with their prized 'foie gras' liver. For the cook, to eat foie gras fresh or in terrine is only the beginning, as Vicky Jones describes so vividly in one of the most absorbing chapters of this most thorough book.

It was in the Dordogne, on my very first visit to France, that I first tasted *confit*, the dish devised by local cooks to use up the meat of fattened foie gras birds. I still remember the delicious morsel that seemed to taste of ham, but a ham far more delicious than anything my native Yorkshire had ever produced. A decade later I learned how to salt the meat, then bake it gently in fat until it is tender enough to fall apart and can be literally *confit*, or preserved for months in a cool place. And I still don't understand why *confit* has remained limited to south-west France, at least until very recently.

Also to be enjoyed in the Dordogne are more modest products such as walnuts and aromatic cold-pressed walnut oil, wild chestnuts (*châtaignes*), wild mushrooms including ceps and chanterelles, fresh white *coco* kidney beans, prunes from Agen and oysters from Bordeaux. As for the dishes, Vicky Jones invites us to explore the mysteries of *miques*, *millassou*, *flaugnarde* and *enchaud*. *Cracquou*, a puff pastry flavoured with lard, was new to me, though I did know that *pastis* in Dordogne has nothing to do with the anise spirit.

No wonder the British flock to the Dordogne, myself included. The food is delicious, the scenery spectacular, and underlying all is the sense of history, of knights in armour, Plantagenet kings, and sturdy settlers repelling all invaders from their fortified *bastides*, the model towns of the thirteenth and fourteenth centuries. Vicky Jones admirably captures past and present in **Dordogne Gastronomique**. Her portraits of auberges, boulangeries, charcuteries, foie gras farms and the people who run them are a compelling evocation of the rural France we all so appreciate, and are anxious to preserve.

ABOVE A fisherman's barque on the Dordogne near Lalinde. Until the construction of the Canal de Lalinde in the 1840s, this part of the river was a hazard for navigation, due to the presence of dangerous rapids.
RIGHT The house of Godard, based in Gourdon, is one of the few companies which guarantees that its foie gras is produced in south-west France, not imported. Godard boutiques are to be found all over Périgord and Quercy, selling not only preserved foie gras, but confit, *pâté*, rillettes *and other local delicacies.*

INTRODUCTION

Pinned on the wall at the Museum of Rural Life near Monflanquin is an extract from a poem written by Paul Valéry that embodies the philosophy of the museum's dedicated curator, Pierre Boissière:

> *L'idée du passé*
> *ne prend un sens*
> *et ne constitue une valeur*
> *que pour les hommes*
> *qui trouve en eux-mêmes*
> *une passion pour l'avenir**

Pierre Boissière is an energetic man, whose interest in the past, like that of Paul Valéry, stems not from mere nostalgia, but from a passionate concern for the future of rural France, and especially for the region of the Dordogne. His mission has many aims: to save old French apple varieties, which would otherwise disappear, lost to a mountain of Golden Delicious; to grow forgotten strains of rye, and show children how to make music from a flute cut from its straw; to record on film how, until recently, prunes were dried in wood-fired ovens, how river fish were trapped and caught, how hemp was grown and made into cloth, and how bricks were made from clay. After a couple of hours at his small and desperately under-funded museum, you come away with a sense of the extraordinary self-sufficiency of these *paysans*, of the pride they took in their work, and their independence of spirit. Naturally, these thoughts lead to the present, and to the future.

During the course of our travels through the Dordogne, we often had the feeling that we, too, were recording a way of life that will have disappeared in ten years' time. The last surviving generation of peasant farmers will be dead, and their disillusioned children, unable or unwilling to scrape a living from a small mixed farm, will probably have moved to the city. Inevitably, the countryside will change for ever, and a significant source of good traditional food, the basis of the recipes in this book, will be lost.

*The significance of the past only has any meaning or value for people who find in themselves a passion for the future.

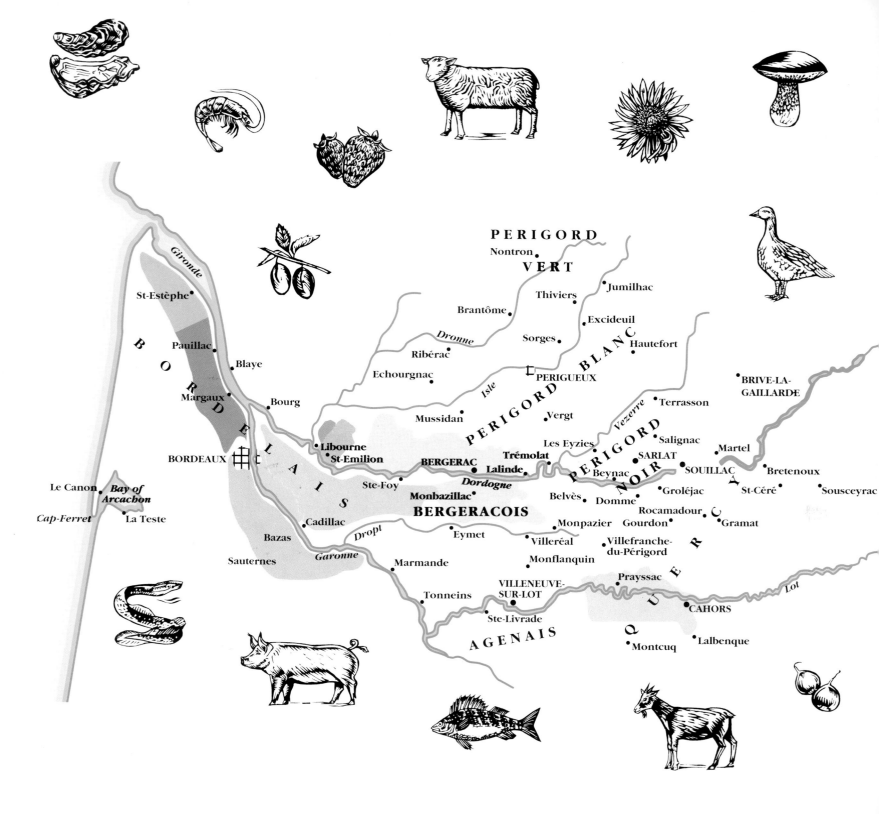

WINE REGIONS

Médoc

Haut-Médoc

Entre-Deux-Mers

Graves

Premières Côtes de Bordeaux

St-Emilion and its satellites

Pomerol

Cahors

Bergerac

One of the most pleasurable aspects of life in the Dordogne, even if you are just a visitor, is a trip to the weekly produce market, held in almost every small town. In summer, trestle tables are laden with strawberries and cherries, courgette flowers and all kinds of salad leaves, making an irresistible display of vivid colours; in autumn, there are walnuts, ceps, chestnuts and the new season's prunes; in winter come the *marchés au gras*, where fattened ducks and geese, with their precious pale yellow livers, are sold alongside black truffles. The backbone of these markets is the group of *petits producteurs*, the smallholders; they sell only what is in season and grown locally, and yet the variety and quality of their goods can be extraordinary. Without them, these markets will not survive, and people will shop in supermarkets, buying plastic-wrapped food that may have been produced thousands of miles away.

This change has far-reaching implications that are already familiar elsewhere: huge container lorries hurtling along country roads, taking food from Spain to England, from Poland to France, and from France to Germany; fruit that is tasteless because it must be picked unripe in order to survive the long journey; cheese that never matures because shelf-life is more important than flavour; and supermarket shelves displaying a vast, bewildering choice of anonymous produce that is neither seasonal nor regional.

Genuine local cooking is in danger of becoming a myth, a marketing ploy exploited by industrial producers to persuade us to buy their expensive ready-made meals. Most of the recipes in this book evolved not from choice, but from necessity: to make a soup with nothing but an egg and a few cloves of garlic (*tourin*), for example; to cook a joint of meat over the open fire (*enchaud*, or *gigot d'agneau à la couronne d'ail*); or to add a touch of acidity before lemons were available (*poulet au verjus, truite au verjus*). The cuisine of the Dordogne is all the richer for it. These dishes could not have been invented by somebody who did all their shopping in a supermarket and cooked in a microwave oven.

Traditional recipes also arose from the peasants' ability to make use of everything edible. In the past, to waste anything was considered almost sinful. Home-made aperitifs were, and still are, flavoured with the leaves of walnut and fruit trees; stale bread was used to thicken soup; delicious salads were made from wild lambs' lettuce, dandelion and cress; ducks' gizzards were transformed into a tasty ragout. Bread itself was made, not by adding shop-bought yeast at each baking, but by saving a bit of the fermenting dough for the next batch, then rising it slowly, at its own pace. Every farm had its own small vineyard and made its own wine. Wild mushrooms – not just ceps, but *mousserons* (fairy-ring mushrooms), *oronges*, *russules* and *trompettes de la mort* (the poor man's truffle) – were gathered and enjoyed.

With a dozen geese, the farmer's wife could provide all of the cooking fat for the household, and make a good profit by selling the foie gras, or fattened livers, for Christmas and New Year celebrations. The rest of the bird was made into *confit*, which would keep for many months in its own fat in an earthenware jar or *toupine*. Most families also had a pig, which conveniently ate all of the vegetable peelings and scraps, and then provided hams, bacon and sausages for the months to come, as well as cooking fat. There was no waste.

Nobody wants to go back to cooking over an open fire, or hoeing the fields by hand, but there are many lessons to be learned from the past. Filled with enthusiastic ideas about sustainable agriculture and concern for the environment, a small but growing number of people, mostly urban refugees, are going back to the land. Growing organic vegetables, making goats' cheese, baking sourdough bread, or cooking regional specialities in *ferme-auberges*, they are united in their belief in the future, and in their ability to produce high-quality food.

Coupled with this belief is a conviction that many of the old, patient ways of doing things are probably still the best. Planting traditional varieties of fruit, for example, which are well suited to the local climate, results in stronger trees with greater resistance to disease than the new high-yield varieties, and so fewer pesticides are needed. Happily, more and more consumers are becoming interested in the diversity of these rare and ancient varieties, too, and are appreciating the superior flavours of their fruit. Among the new breed of farmers are followers of the biodynamic movement, who plant and harvest according to the phases of the moon, as the peasants used to do, and reject the use of chemical fertilizers or pesticides; today, a small band of wine-makers are turning to these methods, with great success.

Long-forgotten ingredients such as verjuice, the juice of sour green grapes, are now being made again, adding variety and interest to regional cooking. After decades of decline, truffle harvests are growing steadily, now that the new *trufficulteurs* of Périgord and Quercy have realized that truffle oaks need careful tending to be productive (as they were at the turn of the century, when the truffle business was at its peak). A recent project to clean up the rivers and install special fish ladders is enabling the fish to come back, and salmon are once again swimming up the Dordogne. Quite surprisingly, research has shown that both goose fat and walnut oil, staple ingredients in the cuisine of Périgord and Quercy, are relatively low in saturated fat, and that the people of a typical region of south-western France were found to have the lowest rates of heart disease in the world after Japan.

Clearly, there is no question of turning back the clock, but experience shows that elements of the less intensive, more environmentally friendly way of family farming practised in this part of France for centuries are worth saving. Without these smallholders, we will be left with an empty landscape – *un paysage sans paysans* – without grain-fed, free-range chickens, hand-made *cabécou* cheeses, sourdough bread, and vegetables that are worth eating, and without the rural culture that produces them. The Dordogne has largely escaped industrialization: it still has small farms, artisan food producers and genuine *produits du terroir*.

These are precisely the features which attract so many outsiders to the region, and, in addition to thousands of summer visitors, the population of the Dordogne now includes a considerable number of British people, eager to snap up crumbling farm buildings as they become vacant, and restore them with loving care. The English are no strangers in this part of the world: ever since the days of Eleanor of Aquitaine, they have felt at home in its gentle countryside and unspoilt villages. Today, it is a living reminder of how England used to be, when watermills ground the corn and bread was baked in wood-fired ovens. Having witnessed the effects of large-scale urbanization in their own country, they have chosen instead to live in a place where the traditions of rural life survive.

Sometimes, as Paul Valéry suggested, the way forward is to take stock of the past: to respect its traditions, not just out of nostalgia, but with an eye to the future. Frequently, it is the simple things in life that give most pleasure, and the rich, varied and rustic cuisine of this region of France is surely something to be treasured.

In small towns or villages, markets are held once a week, while larger towns such as Bergerac or Périgueux have them twice-weekly. In Bergerac, Wednesday is the day for buying flowers, while on Saturday, people shop for food. Bordeaux supports daily food markets - Les Capucins and the ultra-modern Galerie des Grands Hommes - as well as a weekly marché écologique in Place Saint-Pierre and a marché fermier in Place Saint-Michel.

The market is the place to buy local produce, much of it home-grown and freshly-gathered that morning, displayed on trestle tables. These small producers may not have much variety in what they offer, but the quality can be outstanding.

Alongside the petits producteurs, vast mobile shops arrive, all chrome and glass, selling sparkling fresh fish, ripe cheeses from every part of France, or charcuterie from the mountains of Auvergne or the Pyrennees.

ABOVE *Maize and sunflower fields, brown in winter and intersected by lines of poplar trees, form chequerboard patterns in the Dordogne valley near Domme.*
RIGHT *Traditionally, a small boxwood mallet is used for cracking open walnut shells.*
FAR RIGHT *Grey Toulouse geese at La Domaine de Barbe, near Badefols-sur-Dordogne, graze in the fields for most of their six-month lifespan. At the age of 5 months, they are force-fed between 3 and 5 times daily to produce foie gras.*

TOP *Freshly-caught zander* (le sandre),
*or pike-perch, together with a few bream in a
Dordogne fishing boat. The pike-perch is neither
pike nor perch, and is greatly prized for its lean,
white flesh and lack of irritating small bones.
Bream is bony and used for soup.*
ABOVE *Tobacco leaves hanging up to dry in
a well-ventilated wooden barn. Dordogne
is the largest tobacco-producing
department in France, and most of the production
is concentrated in the flat lowlands
of Périgord Noir.*

PERIGORD NOIR

For centuries, the legendary rich cuisine of the Périgord Noir, based on foie gras, truffles and ceps, has been a source of fascination to many a far-flung city-dweller. For those who dream of fine regional cooking it is the ultimate *cuisine du terroir*, born of a land where the traditions of the past are still alive, and where you can eat cheaply and well. The food is not the only irresistible attraction, however. With its picturesque villages, majestic castles, prehistoric sites and wide rivers, the landscape seems fresh from a fairytale, and it has more historic buildings than any other part of France apart from Paris.

During the early years of this century, as the reputation of *périgourdin* gastronomy spread throughout France, inns and *auberges* opened up to feed the travelling gourmets. These restaurants usually had only one menu, of simple but wholesome dishes. The cooks were ordinary women, inspired more by the desire to please the people they were feeding than by the drive to make money or to impress. Word of these provincial *auberges* spread, fuelled by food writers such as Curnonsky, the self-styled 'Prince of Gastronomes'. In the 1920s, he described the cuisine of Périgord as '*sans beurre et sans reproche*' (referring to the ubiquitous use of goose fat in cooking – without butter and without equal – and playing simultaneously on the words of the phrase '*sans peur et sans reproche*', the medieval ideal of the chivalrous knight). On another occasion, Curnonsky referred to Périgord as '*une des régions de notre pays où l'on mange le mieux, et depuis des siècles*', commenting on its long-standing tradition of excellent food. By the 1980s, the Périgord Noir had become one of France's most popular tourist attractions and it now draws many thousands of visitors every year.

The historic market town of Sarlat, with its grand Gothic and Renaissance houses, narrow medieval streets and Saturday market, has long been regarded as the centre of *périgourdin* gastronomy. Carefully restored as a result of a conservation project which began in 1964, its magnificent buildings of golden stone now house expensive shops and restaurants, all advertising *produits du terroir* (regional specialities). At the height of the season the town fills with holidaymakers and suffers from acute traffic problems, while in winter the old quarter is all but deserted, an empty shell awaiting the next influx.

Nevertheless, Sarlat retains a certain vitality. The Saturday market continues to thrive, although there are now relatively few *petits producteurs*, and in summer, vendors of cheap clothes, trinkets and hardware jostle for space with the food sellers. The town boasts a

BASTIDES

During the wars between England and France in the 12th and 13th centuries, the Dordogne became a dividing line in the conflict. Both sides tried to consolidate the hold on their territory by constructing bastides, *such as Monpazier (seen above), Villeréal and Eymet. These new towns, some of which were fortified, were built by pioneering settlers lured by generous incentives, including exemption from military service. All the towns were built to a strict grid pattern, with the principal buildings grouped around a central square, where shady arcades overlooked a covered wooden market. The grid layout ensured that the land was shared out in equal parts, and each family was given an allotment on the town's outskirts for a kitchen garden, and another plot in the surrounding countryside to grow crops. Citizens also had the right to sell their produce in the covered market place.*

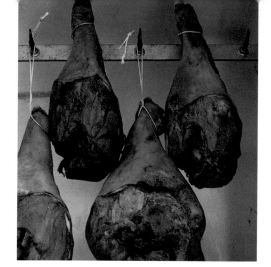

LEFT *Local produce on sale at the market in Sarlat. A special licence is needed to sell wild mushrooms.*
ABOVE *Eau-de-vie distilled from plums is aged in oak casks at La Salamandre, a small family-run distillery just outside Sarlat.*
RIGHT *Goats' cheeses, flavoured with wild thyme and juniper berries, on sale at the market in Domme.*

COUNTRY HAM FROM DOMME

The bastide town of Domme is built over limestone caves, and the dry air provides perfect conditions for making ham. La Boucherie Lambert makes the most of its location, with doors that extend across the entire front of the building, so that the shop is open to the air. Whole hams hang from the ceiling over the counter and above the ancient, wooden-fronted refrigerator. On market day, a queue of customers waits patiently while each purchase is discussed in great detail, then meticulously wrapped. Madame Lambert takes the money at a marble-topped desk by her side, and receives telephone orders at the same time. Jambon de pays, which is cured and eaten raw, is their speciality. The hams are salted, then covered with cloth and stacked in special bins with a layer of oak ash over the top, 'pour donner un parfum', where they stay for 40 days. Then they are dried for a whole year, hanging in the shop in the free flow of air. Each ham has initials cut out of the skin – 'BL' – by the Lamberts' son, Bernard, who does it for fun, to while away winter days.

number of excellent pâtisseries, notably Maison Vergne, where the finest *gâteaux aux noix* – moist, light and coated in dark chocolate – are to be found. Alain Bazin, *artisan chocolatier* in the Avenue de la République, coats his walnut tarts with coffee icing, and makes exquisite chocolate-covered *pruneaux fourrés*, and jewel-like *pâtes de fruits*. If you want a traditional meal, guaranteed to be both rich and satisfying, look no further than the Saint-Albert restaurant in the Place Pasteur.

Another Sarlat institution is Jackie Porret's fishing shop and bar, in the Place des Oies. Jackie Porret is a genial, bespectacled wine connoisseur and fisherman, who inherited the bar from his father, and has made no attempt to modernize or enlarge it. With only one table, unpredictable opening hours and no guarantee that any food will be served, it is reassuringly uncommercial. One thing is certain, though – good wine will be on offer.

FOIE GRAS

Window-shopping in Sarlat, you soon become aware that buying a local delicacy such as foie gras is not just a question of making a simple purchase; it is a matter of enormous complexity. For a start, it may come as a surprise to see entire shops devoted solely to the sale of very expensive canned food. As well as plain foie gras, there is *bloc de foie gras, pâté de foie, mousse de foie, crème de foie, parfait de foie gras, purée de foie, cou farci au foie gras, even mousse-purée.* Then there is the choice of goose or duck foie gras and a bewildering number of producers, too: Delpeyrat, Rougié, G.A. Besse, Champion, Godard – all the big names are

there, plus many other less familiar ones. A market stall has fresh foie gras to sell, either raw and vacuum-packed in plastic, or *mi-cuit*, (lightly cooked), as well as the usual conserves in tins. Which to choose?

In the past, foie gras was a luxury food, produced on small farms to be consumed by a privileged élite, but over the past few years it has become increasingly mass-produced and mass-marketed. Much of the foie gras sold in cans by large producers – perhaps 50 per cent – does not come from south-west France at all, but is imported in its raw state from Israel, Hungary, Bulgaria and Poland, to be processed and canned under French labels. It may taste no different from local foie gras, but visitors in search of the genuine Périgord product may feel cheated and prefer something unquestionably authentic.

In November 1992, in order to counter the deteriorating public image of foie gras, a group of seven producers from the south-west formed the Comité Renaissance, with its own charter of standards governing the origin, quality, methods of production and processing of their products. With the backing of famous chefs such as Alain Senderens, André Daguin, Michel Guérard, Alain Dutournier and Alexis Pélissou, who meet regularly and conduct blind tastings, the committee has considerable authority. Two members of the Comité Renaissance, Godard at Gourdon, and Roger Crouzel at Salignac, are based in the Dordogne; the others are from the Landes and Gers regions.

Roger Crouzel is an *artisan conservier*, a relatively small producer, who does not raise ducks and geese himself, but prepares and cooks a wide range of conserves, pâtés and *confits* in the traditional way, subject to strict EC hygiene regulations. A former chef who trained at such illustrious establishments as Le Tour d'Argent and Le Crillon in Paris, he guarantees that his produce is genuinely south-western in origin. He is a stickler for high quality, and he personally selects the goose livers from the co-operative in Sarlat. Duck livers come either from the co-operative at Thiviers, or from the Landes. Out of choice, he does much of his business by mail order, and has built up a faithful clientèle over the past 20 years.

One way to be certain of the quality of what you are buying is to go to a reliable *artisan conservier* such as Roger Crouzel; another is to buy direct from a recommended farm or producer, such as Domaine de Barbe (see page 19). Alternatively, fresh, raw goose or duck foie gras can be bought from the farmers' co-operative in the old abattoir on the outskirts of Sarlat.

In Périgord, where birds are fed on yellow maize (rather than white, as they are in the Landes) a good foie gras can be recognized by its uniform yellow ochre colour. It should also be supple to the touch, even when taken straight from the refrigerator – this suppleness is a better mark of quality than mere weight, for it indicates that the liver is not too fatty, and so will not melt excessively when it is cooked. A fattened goose liver generally weighs about 800g/1¾lb, while a duck liver is roughly half that. Neither should have a pronounced smell.

Raw foie gras is very delicate and can easily be ruined by over-cooking, so most people prefer to buy it *mi-cuit* or in *semi-conserve*. In this state it is cooked and ready for eating, but it must be kept refrigerated and consumed within about three weeks. (If pasteurized and cooked in sealed glass jars or tins, however, *mi-cuit* will keep for six months or longer in the refrigerator.) More succulent and tender than sterilized foie gras in tins, *mi-cuit* is generally only available during winter, and spoils too easily to be bought by mail order.

LE DOMAINE DE BARBE

At le Domaine de Barbe, near Badefols-sur-Dordogne, Michel Kuster (above) and his son Pierre-Yves raise ducks and geese on their farm, and have a commercial kitchen, or laboratoire, where they make their own conserves. They buy day-old ducklings and goslings, which live in a heated barn (centre left) until the weather is warm enough for them to go outside to the fields. There they stay, grazing happily, until they are ready for gavage, the process of force-feeding. While this might be anathema to most British people, the French argue that geese and ducks are migratory birds and are therefore naturally predisposed to stuff themselves in preparation for a long journey without food.

For geese, gavage starts at five months, while ducks are sufficiently mature at four months. Ducks are force-fed on maizemeal porridge twice a day for two weeks before they are slaughtered, while geese eat between three and six times daily for three weeks, consuming about a kilogram (2lb) of maize a day.

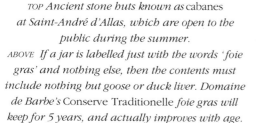

TOP Ancient stone huts known as cabanes at Saint-André d'Allas, which are open to the public during the summer.

ABOVE If a jar is labelled just with the words 'foie gras' and nothing else, then the contents must include nothing but goose or duck liver. Domaine de Barbe's Conserve Traditionelle foie gras will keep for 5 years, and actually improves with age.

At the marchés au gras, *goose and duck livers
(above) are sold alongside the flattened-out
carcasses, which are called* paletots, *or overcoats.
Held throughout the winter, fat poultry
markets are at their busiest in the run-up to
Christmas and New Year.*

Without doubt, the most convenient way to buy foie gras is in a tin, especially if you have a long journey ahead of you before you can eat it. Tinned foie gras products are subject to very strict labelling regulations, and it is useful to know that any label bearing the words '*foie gras entier*' indicates that the contents contain nothing but whole lobes, or pieces of lobe, of goose or duck liver. This is the top of the range, and likely to be very expensive. '*Foie gras d'oie*' and '*foie gras de canard*' also contain nothing but the liver, but may be composed of quite small pieces pressed together. '*Bloc de foie gras*' also contains only foie gras, but it is basically an emulsified purée of pieces of duck or goose liver, reconstituted by machine, so it is considerably cheaper. Still further down the ladder are parfaits, which must contain at least 75 per cent foie gras; then there are pâtés, galantines and purées, which can contain as little as 50 per cent, made up with forcemeat, eggs and other ingredients; and finally there are other products labelled '*au foie d'oie*' or '*au foie de canard*', which state the amount of foie gras on the label.

A terrine of foie gras is generally served at the beginning of the meal, cool but not too cold (it should be taken out of the refrigerator ten minutes before serving), with toasted white bread or brioche, and a glass of chilled, sweet white wine – wines such as Monbazillac, Saussignac, Barsac, Sauternes or Loupiac would be served in this part of France. Some people prefer to partner it with red wine, but this is unusual. If you have bought raw foie gras, you can, of course, cook it fresh and serve it hot (see pages 28–9). For the greatest treat, sauté the foie gras quickly and serve it with warm slices of apple or pear, and with the pan juices deglazed with sweet wine.

Périgord Noir built its fame on the goose, and in the past, every small farm raised a dozen or so, as much for the fat, which was the basis of all cooking, as for the liver, which could be sold on to the local doctor, lawyer or schoolteacher for a good price. Even today, the goose predominates in this region, and the co-operative at Sarlat sells hardly any ducks. (By contrast, the Thiviers co-operative, in the north of the Dordogne region, deals mainly in ducks.) Geese are far more difficult to raise, and it is easy to understand why so many farms have gone over to the fattening of ducks instead of geese. With the ever-increasing popularity of *magret de canard* (fattened duck breast), the profits to be made on ducks are correspondingly greater. The choice of goose or duck liver is a matter of taste; goose liver has more finesse, while some prefer the fuller flavour of *foie gras de canard*.

Autumn and winter are the high seasons in the gastronomic year, for this is when ceps make their appearance, when walnuts fall from the trees, and later on, in November, the *marchés au gras*, or fattened poultry markets, take place in the run-up to Christmas and the New Year. At this time of year, several of the farms in Périgord Noir offer short courses in making traditional conserves from fattened geese. At their farm in the woods near Meyrals, Elie and Pierrette Coustaty demonstrate to visitors the traditional skills of converting a goose into *confit*, *pâté*, *cou farci*, *grattons* and foie gras, and each person leaves at the end of their three-day stay with the results of their labour. The added attraction of a *séjour* at the Coustaty farm is the food – not just the poultry, but the fresh vegetables from the garden, and huge loaves of freshly baked *pain au levain* (sourdough bread) from the wood-fired oven at the bottom of the garden.

A terrine of foie gras, the ultimate luxury, is usually served cold at the beginning of a meal, with a sweet white wine such as Monbazillac, Sauternes or Loupiac, and toasted brioche or bread. However, some prefer the more robust flavour of red wine as an accompaniment.

THE NOBLE WALNUT

One of the most remarkable features of the landscape in the Périgord Noir is the number of walnut groves. The handsome trees provide a canopy of dappled shade in summer and a valuable harvest in early October, when the husks split open and the fresh, ripe nuts fall to the ground. The Sarladais has always been famous for walnuts, but the trees are now seen all over Périgord, especially in the area around Molières and Belvès.

It is said that with the walnut, nothing is wasted except the sound of the shell being cracked open. In spring, tender young leaves are gathered and infused in red wine to make *quinquina*, or *vin de noyer*, an astringent aperitif much appreciated as an appetite stimulant. Later on, people pick the unripe walnuts and macerate them in eau-de-vie to make a digestive that enjoys the dubious reputation of being able to 'kill worms and cure jaundice'. Green walnuts can also be made into jam, or even pickled, English-style.

René Carrier and his wife Christine live in the bastide village of Molières, and grow walnuts commercially. It was their idea to tempt the sizeable local English population with a taste of their homeland, and so they started to make pickled walnuts. The perfect accompaniment to cold meats and charcuterie, the pickled walnuts proved to be very popular with their French neighbours, but to the Carriers' surprise, the English remain unenthusiastic. Their home-made *confit de noix*, a sweetened paste of walnuts, has more universal appeal, however, either spread on bread at breakfast-time or used in baking, cutting out half the work of

making *la tarte aux noix*, for example. Salted, toasted walnuts and other delicacies are on the agenda for the future, and the Carriers already produce walnut oil, which they sell at the farm gate. Like so many of their fellow farmers, they have found that simply growing and selling produce is no longer enough to make a living, and have been propelled into the business of food processing and running *chambres d'hôtes*. Despite all the hard work, they enjoy the opportunity to explain local customs to visitors at their dinner table; *le chabrol*, for example, which involves pouring red wine into the last dregs of soup left in the bowl, to warm the wine and get a heady rush of alcohol.

Although mechanical walnut harvesters, and drying and shelling machines exist, most of these tasks are still performed by hand in Périgord Noir, and involve whole families, from children to grandparents. The job of breaking open the shells with a boxwood hammer is one usually reserved for old people, who take pride in the number of kernels they manage to extract whole. The skill lies in knowing exactly where to hit the shell, and it is worth acquiring, because whole kernels sell at a premium, while broken ones, known as *arlequins* or *invalides*, fetch less and will probably be made into oil.

Walnut oil, apart from imparting a distinctive flavour to salads and vegetables (see page 33) is known to be good for one's general health, being high in beneficial polyunsaturated fats and low in saturated fats. Le Moulin de la Tour, a watermill at Sainte-Nathalène dating from the sixteenth century, is run by Urbain Tache, whose robust good health in his later years makes him a walking advertisement for his product. The mill opens daily for the sale of walnut oil, but it is best to go on Fridays when the process can be seen in action.

OPPOSITE ABOVE The austere 13th-century castle at Beynac, seen through a field of maize stalks.
OPPOSITE BELOW Arnaud Carrier, his hands stained with black juice after gathering walnuts at the family farm in Molières. His son René now runs the farm (above), and makes walnut oil and confit de noix.
RIGHT Walnut oil is often sold straight from the vat, and put into recycled beer or wine bottles.
FAR RIGHT (above) Les Arlequines de Carlux - toasted walnuts, coated with bitter chocolate, and dredged in cocoa - made at le Domaine de Béquignol, near Carlux. The shop is also the source of an excellent aperitif, Béquinoix, made out of ripe walnut kernels. Unlike traditional vin de noyer, which is made by macerating walnut leaves in alcohol, it has no bitterness and actually tastes of walnuts.
(Below) Walnut tart is sometimes coated with dark bitter chocolate.

THE WALNUT
MARKET, BELVES

*Every Wednesday morning during October and
November, farmers with only a few sacks of
walnuts to sell take them to the wholesale market
in the hilltop village of Belvès, held under the
old covered* halles *in the Place d'Armes.
Golden light floods the square, as sacks of
walnuts are unloaded on the cobbled floor of the
market place, and propped up against the
stone columns that support the massive oak roof
timbers. Hessian flour sacks, brown paper
sacks and even plastic fertilizer sacks are used to
hold the walnuts. At the beginning of the
season, the nuts are still wet and heavy; these*
petits producteurs *do not have their own
mechanical dryers, relying instead on the sun, but
when sun is in short supply, they must sell
their walnuts wet, and accept lower prices. Some
people have only two bags to sell, others as
many as eight, each weighing about 45kg/100lb.
As the wholesalers arrive in their big white
vans, the buzz of conversation mounts and prices
are heatedly discussed. The sacks are untied
and their contents displayed as the
church bell strikes ten. At this stage,
the wholesalers move from one grower to the next,
plunging their hands into the sacks,
cracking open shells, haggling over
the price. By 10.20am virtually all of the
walnuts have been sold, but the
mood of the growers is understandably subdued.
For despite the freshness and fine flavour
of these walnuts, prices have dropped
drastically due to the influx of cheaper imported
walnuts from California.*

MUSHROOM MADNESS

There are few things that make a *Périgourdin* angry, but one of them is the thought that people from the Corrèze or the Bordelais might be stealing their ceps. If your car's registration plates bear the numbers 19 or 33, it is extremely unwise to park it in a wood during the mushroom season, as you run the risk of having the tyres punctured; for although gathering a few for the family is considered acceptable, filling up the car boot is not, and retaliation is the order of the day.

Boletus edulis, the penny bun or *porcini*, is the one everyone is after. Most common of the edible ceps, it is characterized by its velvety brown cap, creamy-coloured, spongy pores and bulbous stem, which is nearly as good to eat as the cap. As the mushroom gets older, the colour of the spores becomes yellow-green. Unlike some varieties of boletus, which turn bright blue when cut, this one does not discolour. Even finer, though rarer, is the prized *tête de nègre*, which has, as its name suggests, a darker cap, almost black. Poisonous ceps can be recognized by their orange-red spores, but amateurs should always get an expert to identify their finds before tucking in. In France, pharmacies offer this service.

Rather conveniently for the mushroom-gatherer, ceps grow in symbiosis with certain kinds of tree, usually chestnuts, oaks or hornbeams, which gives a clue to good hunting grounds.

RIGHT Gilbert Ricoux, returning from the woods near Groléjac with a prized tête de nègre *mushroom, a type of cep which is recognizable by its black cap and white spores. Experienced mushroom-hunters like Gilbert can often find ceps by using their sense of smell, combined with an intuitive knowledge of the forest.*

But even when told exactly where to look, it is astonishing how an untrained eye can miss the treasure while the experts haul in basket-loads of edible fungi.

Villefranche-du-Périgord, the most ancient of *périgourdin* bastides, is the scene of an extraordinary cep market. Ceps generally make their appearance in August and September, but only after rain and only if the weather is warm enough, so the exact dates of these markets are never announced in advance. The *syndicat d'initiative* can usually be relied upon to know, though only on the day. The market takes place under the timbered *halles*, at the sound of a bell that rings at precisely 4 pm. Only local landowners are allowed to sell ceps at Villefranche, and the mushrooms must have been gathered on their own land. This not only ensures that ceps bought here are genuinely *du terroir*, it also prevents the mayhem that would otherwise ensue during *la belle saison* – the chestnut forests around Villefranche are stuffed full of ceps, and a free-for-all would be intolerable. Ardent ceps fans may want to take a break from mushroom-hunting to visit the small, old-fashioned Museum of Ceps and Chestnuts, which has erratic opening hours. It is housed in the *syndicat d'initiative*, in the main street of Villefranche.

Although nothing can beat *cèpes farcies* (see page 33) or an *omelette aux cèpes* made with freshly gathered mushrooms, ceps are obligingly easy to preserve, and can be enjoyed all year round. During the season, the aroma of ceps sizzling in the pan fills every kitchen in Périgord Noir, as cooks are busy bottling them in large glass *bocaux*, which are then stored away for the future. Ceps can also be frozen, although they then have a tendency to become rather slimy. Dried ceps retain their flavour very well and are good for casseroles and *daubes* but are not suitable for eating on their own.

DAILY BREAD

Périgord's gastronomic reputation may have been built on the foie gras, truffles and game enjoyed by the aristocracy, but for most of the peasants such luxuries were to be sold, not consumed. In the past, their diet consisted largely of bread and soup; in some cases, it still does. So it is no surprise that soup should be the forte of the *périgourdin* cook, with a repertoire covering all seasons and all manner of ingredients. Except in the smartest restaurants, soup begins every meal, even today, and is sometimes so substantial that it is a struggle to plough through subsequent courses. Dried haricot beans often form the main ingredient of these robust dishes, combined with carrots, potatoes, leeks, sorrel (see page 31) or whatever can be found in the vegetable garden. Soup is always accompanied by, or poured over, thick slices of coarse country bread, a custom which is a reminder of the days when bread was baked only once a week, and eventually became so hard that it needed a thorough soaking to make it edible.

Although few people still bake at home, good bread is not hard to find. The best bread in Sarlat comes from Père Pauliac at the Boulangerie de la Gare, whose *pain du seigle*, baked on Wednesdays, is famous throughout the region. The hearty *soupe paysanne* served at La Ferme Escalier, a popular country auberge in the nearby village of Montfort, is thickened with Père Pauliac's rye bread and is so solid that you can stand a spoon up in it.

When in search of traditional country bread, look out for the sign '*pain au levain, cuit au feu de bois*', as this signifies the authentic sourdough loaf that was the staple food of the peasants until recently. For country people, using sourdough was the only practical method of baking when yeast was not available, but its slightly sour taste and moist, creamy crumb has such appeal that the method lives on. After each baking, a small amount of dough, *la mère*, is kept back and used as the starter for the next batch of bread. Freshly milled flour and a slow rising make loaves that keep fresh for a week, unlike the factory-made bread of today, which is stale within hours.

One or two old-timers still bake bread exactly as it was done in the past, burning faggots of wood to heat the outdoor oven. René Neuville, who lives on a farm deep in the countryside near La Cassagne, is one such enthusiast. At about four or five in the afternoon, his huge round *tourtes* of sourdough bread, each weighing two kilograms (4lb), are taken from the wood-fired oven in the farmyard, and customers arrive from all directions to buy. Not far away, at Meyrals, Père Coustaty bakes for his family and the people staying at their *ferme-*

Surrounded by woodland, the village of Urval possesses a number of picturesque houses and a small fortified church dating from the 11th century. This cottage of honey-coloured stone with a steeply-pitched tiled roof is typically périgourdin in design.

auberge, kneading the dough by hand and rising it in huge hand-hewn dishes of poplar. His oven is over a hundred years old, and has been in continuous use since it was built.

An alternative to bread is *mique* (see page 34), a huge dumpling poached in broth, and served with *petit salé* (salt pork), casseroles, *confits* and salads. Every Thursday, Lalande, *traiteur-charcutier* of Sarlat, makes *miques*, and they are much appreciated by his regular customers as they are thought to be difficult to make well. Admittedly, the off-white, pasty balls do not look very appealing, but *miques* taste surprisingly good, especially if flavoured with bits of ham or bacon. They are even better the next day, sliced and toasted or fried.

La bouillie de maïs, a maizemeal porridge rather like Italian *polenta*, is another traditional accompaniment to stews. It can be eaten as it is, or poured when hot on to a greased board, left to cool, then cut into squares, brushed with beaten egg and dredged in flour, and fried in goose fat until crisp and brown. Prepared in this way, the dish is known as *rimottes*.

LE VIEUX LOGIS

TREMOLAT, TEL 53 22 80 06

The sleepy village of Trémolat lies amid fields of tobacco and maize, partly encircled by a meander in the Dordogne river. In this peaceful setting stands the Vieux Logis, one of the prettiest and most luxurious hotels in the region. Furnished in country style with family antiques, this has been the home of the Giraudel-Destord family for almost 400 years. The old tobacco-drying barn is now a restaurant, while the stable has been tastefully converted into a cosy bar. Outside, orchards, flower-beds and lawns are enclosed by clipped box hedges, and a stream flows through the garden.

An ardent believer in the importance of terroir *and in maintaining the regional identity of Périgord, Bernard Giraudel, the present owner, naturally takes a lively interest in what is going on in the kitchen. Chef Jean-Pierre Duribreux enjoys finding the best of local ingredients – truffles, foie gras, river fish, free-range poultry and fresh vegetables – and creating a menu of the great classic dishes of Périgord around them:* truffe en croûte, tourain blanchi *(see page 56),* cou farci *(goose-neck sausage),* lièvre *(hare)* à la royale, foie gras poêlé *(see below),* millas sarladais, *as well as his own creations.*

FOIE GRAS DE CANARD POELE AUX POIRES ROTIES ET SA SAUCE AU JUS DE TRUFFE

Pan-fried Fresh Duck Foie Gras with Roasted Pears and a Sauce of Truffle Juice

In this mouth-watering dish from Le Vieux Logis, the sweetness of roasted pears provides a perfect foil for the succulent richness of foie gras. The aim is to brown the outside of the duck liver while leaving the inside pink and soft, so have all the ingredients ready before you begin the final stage of cooking, as this only takes a few seconds.

Prepare the pears first, then, while they are cooking, take the duck liver out of the refrigerator in order to devein and slice it. Because the liver contains so much fat it solidifies when chilled, but if left at room temperature for more than half an hour, it will become soft and too floppy to handle. When you have finished preparing it, put it back to chill until you are completely ready. *(Illustrated opposite, above)*

SERVES 4
4 pears (Comice or Williams)
8g/¼oz butter
450g/1lb fresh duck foie gras
oil, for frying

FOR THE SAUCE
100ml/3½fl oz truffle juice
200ml/7fl oz clear veal stock
45g/1½oz cold butter, cut into cubes
salt and freshly ground black pepper

Preheat the oven to 200°C/400°F/gas mark 6. Peel and quarter the pears, removing the stem and core. Melt the butter in a flameproof dish, and brown the pears lightly on each side in the butter. Then place the dish in a hot oven, and continue to cook for about 30 minutes, turning over half-way through cooking, until they are golden brown and cooked through. While the pears are cooking, devein the liver (use a very sharp knife), first scraping off the fine membrane that entirely covers the liver, and then removing all of the bloody veins and sinews, starting at the top and working downwards. Next cut the liver into 4 escalopes, and return the slices to the refrigerator until you are ready to cook.

Lightly brush a frying pan with oil, and when the pan is hot, fry the slices of foie gras for 1 minute on each side, until golden brown. Then quickly remove them from the pan and place on an absorbent cloth. Keep warm while you make the sauce.

Deglaze the pan with truffle juice, then add the veal stock and reduce by boiling over high heat for 5 minutes.

Finally, whisk in the cold cubes of butter, check the seasoning and pass the sauce through a fine sieve. Pour over the slices of foie gras, and serve immediately, with the roasted pears arranged around.

TRUFFE EN CROUTE

Whole Truffles Enveloped in Bacon and Foie Gras, Baked in Pastry

An extremely simple way of combining two of the most highly prized ingredients in French cuisine, this is the dish to start a celebratory meal in great style. Tuber melanosporum, *the legendary black truffle of Périgord and Quercy, is unrivalled for its astonishingly pungent aroma, and even minute scraps of peel are capable of flavouring whole joints of meat or a dozen eggs. At Le Vieux Logis, a whole fresh truffle – the ultimate luxury – is wrapped in thin slices of smoked bacon, enveloped by foie gras, and baked as a kind of pasty, which is served with* sauce Périgueux. *(Illustrated right)*

SERVES 4
900g/2lb puff pastry
4 thin slices of smoked bacon
250g/8½oz fresh duck foie gras
4 black truffles, each weighing about
45g/1½oz, peeled
1 egg, beaten
salt and freshly ground black pepper
600ml/1 pint *sauce Périgueux*, to serve (see page 37)

Preheat the oven to 220°C/425°F/gas mark 7. Divide the pastry into 8 parts, and roll each out as thinly as possible. Cut a circle from each.

Lay 4 of the pastry circles on a greased baking tray, and place a slice of bacon in the centre of each. Cut the foie gras into dice, and divide equally into four, placing a portion on each slice of bacon. Place a truffle on top, season with salt and pepper, and then wrap the bacon over each truffle and portion of foie gras. Brush beaten egg around the borders of the pastry, and top with the remaining 4 circles, pressing down firmly around the edges to seal. Brush with more beaten egg, and bake for 25-30 minutes. Serve immediately, on hot plates, with *sauce Périgueux*.

SOUPE A L'OSEILLE ET AUX HARICOTS

Sorrel and Haricot Bean Soup

As with so many of the traditional country recipes of the Périgord, this satisfying soup-stew is made from a small number of inexpensive ingredients, skilfully combined. The amount of stock or water given in this recipe makes a thick main-course dish; for a lighter soup, increase the amount of liquid. (Illustrated left)

SERVES 4
**225g/8oz dried white beans
1l/1¾pt stock or water
2 garlic cloves, chopped
1 small onion, chopped
sprig of thyme
bay leaf
1tbsp goose fat
1 thick slice smoked bacon, weighing about 85g/3oz, diced
handful of sorrel leaves, shredded
salt and freshly ground black pepper**

Blanch the beans for 5 minutes in boiling water, drain and leave to soak in fresh water for 2 hours. Drain, then bring to the boil in fresh water or stock, together with the garlic, onion, thyme and bay leaf. Simmer gently for an hour or so; the exact length of time will depend on the age of the beans, and they may take longer to reach the point when they start to fall apart.

In another pan, melt the goose fat, and sweat the diced bacon for about 10 minutes. Add the shredded sorrel, and cook gently until reduced to a purée. Add the beans with their cooking liquid, remove the herbs, then lightly mash some of the beans to thicken the soup. Adjust seasoning and serve with crusty bread.

FOIE DE CANARD FRAIS EN TERRINE

Terrine of Fresh Duck Liver

The liver of a fattened duck or goose is very delicate, and can easily be ruined by cooking at too high a temperature, when it will literally melt. For this reason, many people prefer to leave it to the professionals. However, raw, fresh foie gras is much cheaper than canned foie gras entier, and there is extra pleasure in doing it yourself. Fresh foie gras can be bought from the co-operative in Sarlat or Thiviers.

SERVES 4
**400g/14oz fresh raw liver from a fattened duck
1tsp salt
pinch of black pepper
2tsp port
2tsp armagnac**

To prepare the liver, first remove the fine membrane that covers it, using a sharp knife, then cut all traces of green gall bladder away. Next, separate the two lobes with your hands. Remove all blood vessels and white fat or gristle, cutting into the liver if necessary, then press it back together. Sprinkle with the salt and pepper, port and armagnac, and leave to marinate for at least 12 hours in a cool place.

Use a terrine that will be more or less filled by the liver, and pack the liver in it tightly, pressing down firmly to ensure that there are no air pockets. Cover with foil, and allow to return to room temperature before cooking.

Preheat the oven to 120°C/250°F/gas mark ½, and boil some water for a bain-marie. When the oven has reached the right temperature, place the terrine in the bain-marie, pour hot water around it, and cook in the oven for

30–40 minutes. The fat should just be beginning to run from the foie gras, but it should still be pink inside; if the fat has not started to run, cook for a little longer. Leave to cool, then refrigerate for 2 days to become firm.

Serve in slices, chilled, with toasted bread or brioche and chilled Monbazillac or Sauternes.

OEUFS A LA PERIGOURDINE

Périgourdin Stuffed Eggs

This dish uses up leftover bits of chicken, ham or pâté de foie gras to stuff hard-boiled eggs. It epitomizes the périgourdin cooks' ability to invent according to the ingredients at hand.

SERVES 4
**5 eggs
4 heaped tsp of minced cooked chicken or ham, or pâté
a little walnut oil or butter
2tbsp finely chopped herbs
oil or goose fat, for frying**

Hard-boil 4 of the eggs, peel, and cut in half lengthwise. Remove the yolks, and using a fork, mash them with the meat or pâté. Add walnut oil or butter if the meat is not fatty, salt and pepper if necessary, and the chopped herbs. Spoon the mixture back into the halves of egg white, pressing it well down and rounding off the top.

Separate the remaining egg, and lightly whisk the white in a shallow bowl. Heat the fat in the frying-pan, dip each half egg into the white, and put immediately into the hot fat. Fry for about 5 minutes, until brown on both sides, and drain on paper towels. Serve as a snack with aperitifs, or with salad as a first course.

OEUFS BROUILLES AUX TRUFFES

Creamy Scrambled Eggs with Truffles

A deceptively simple first course, the pungent aroma of truffles is offset to perfection by the blandness of eggs, cooked here to a rich, creamy smoothness. If you have fresh truffle, leave it for 24 hours in a bowl with the eggs before cooking them so that they absorb the aroma of truffle. Either fresh or canned truffle can be used; either way, save the peelings for flavouring another dish. (Illustrated right)

SERVES 4
1 black Périgord truffle (*Tuber melanosporum*) peeled
6 eggs
85g/3oz butter
1tbsp thick cream
4 warm individual pastry cases (optional)

With a sharp knife, cut the truffle in half, and thinly slice off 4 rounds, for decorating the finished dish. Cut the remaining truffle into tiny dice. Break the eggs into a bowl, season with a generous pinch of salt, and whisk until light and frothy. Stir in the diced truffle.

The eggs must be cooked very slowly, either in a double boiler, or a heavy pan. Melt the butter in the pan, and pour in the eggs, stirring constantly with a wooden spoon. As the eggs start to thicken at the bottom and sides of the pan, stir them into the centre, so that they mix with the uncooked egg. Cook for about 5 minutes, stirring all the time, until almost done. Take off the heat, continue stirring until cooked, then add the cream. Pour into pastry cases or ramekins, top each serving with a slice of truffle, and serve immediately.

CEPES FARCIS

*Ceps Stuffed with Duck and
Sausage Meat*

*This is a dish for autumn as you need fresh,
fairly large ceps with open caps. The filling can
be varied according to what is available, and
at a pinch, cultivated, brown-cap mushrooms
would be used instead of ceps – but they cannot
match the rich forest flavour of the real thing.*

SERVES 6
12 medium to large ceps
3tbsp fresh white breadcrumbs
2tbsp milk
3 garlic cloves
**170g/6oz cooked duck meat or *confit de
canard***
2tbsp chopped parsley
225g/8oz sausage meat or *rillettes*
4tbsp walnut oil
salt and freshly ground black pepper

Preheat the oven to 200°C/400°F/gas mark 6.
Wipe the ceps, but do not wash them, and cut
off the stalks. Leave the caps whole. Trim the
stalks with a sharp knife, discarding the earthy
base, and chop the rest into small dice.

Soak the breadcrumbs in milk, and squeeze
out the excess. Finely chop 2 of the garlic
cloves and mince or chop the duck meat. In a
large bowl, mix breadcrumbs, parsley, chopped
garlic, duck and sausage meat, and season.

Cut the remaining garlic clove in half, and
rub the cut surfaces over a baking tin or dish
large enough to contain all of the ceps. Drizzle
half of the walnut oil over the base of the dish.
Spoon the filling mixture into the upturned
mushroom caps, and arrange them in the dish.
Sprinkle the rest of the walnut oil over the
mushroom filling. Bake the ceps in the oven
for 30–45 minutes, until the tops are browned
and the mushrooms cooked through. Serve on
its own, or with roast meat or poultry.

POMMES DE TERRE SARLADAISES

*Potatoes Sautéed in Goose Fat
with Garlic and Parsley*

*Crisp and brown on the outside, soft in the
middle, these potatoes are the classic accompaniment to* confit de canard *or roast meat. Some
cooks slice the potatoes thinly, and break them
up slightly towards the end of cooking, others
cut them into chunks and leave them un-
broken. (Illustrated on page 36)*

SERVES 4
675g/1½lb waxy potatoes
2tbsp goose fat
2 garlic cloves, finely chopped
2tbsp chopped parsley

Peel the potatoes, and cut into small chunks or
thin slices. Heat the fat in a frying pan, and put
the potatoes into the hot fat. Season with salt.
Cook over brisk heat for about 10 minutes,
turning over from time to time to brown on all
sides, and taking care not to let them stick.
Turn down the heat, and continue to cook for
another 30 minutes or so, scraping the crisp,
brown bits from the bottom of the pan every
10 minutes, and mixing them in. Sprinkle with
garlic and parsley towards the end of cooking.

HARICOTS VERTS A L'HUILE DE NOIX

*French Beans Dressed with
Walnut Oil*

*One of the delights of early summer is a plate of
young green beans, briefly cooked so that they
retain their crunch and brilliant colour,
dressed with fragrant oil and a small clove of
new season's garlic. (Illustrated on page 36)*

SERVES 4
450g/1lb young French beans
1tbsp walnut oil
1 clove fresh garlic, finely chopped
salt and freshly ground black pepper

Put a large pan of lightly salted water on to
boil, and top and tail the beans. When the
water boils, tip in the beans, and bring quickly
back to the boil. Cook, without covering the
pan, for 5–8 minutes, depending on the size
and age of the beans, then drain and put them
back into the pan. Stir in the walnut oil, garlic
and seasoning, replace the lid, and leave for a
couple of minutes in the warm pan for the
flavours to infuse. Serve immediately, as an
accompaniment to roast or grilled meat.

POULET DE MONTIGNAC AUX LEGUMES VERTS

Roast Chicken with Asparagus, Broad Beans, Peas and French Beans

Montignac is best known for the Lascaux caves, discovered by some local schoolboys in 1940. In common with the other fertile river valleys in the region, the Vézère valley supports many smallholdings, where the ingredients for a Sunday lunch in May could be rustled up from the kitchen garden and farmyard to make a simple, delicious meal like this.

SERVES 4
1 shallot, finely chopped
1 garlic clove, finely chopped
1tbsp goose fat or oil
1tbsp each chopped parsley and tarragon
55g/2oz *jambon de pays* or air-dried ham, diced
1 free-range chicken, weighing about 1.35kg/3lb, with giblets
1 slice white bread
3 thin slices fatty bacon
115g/4oz each fresh green asparagus, broad beans (shelled weight), peas (shelled weight) and French beans
salt and freshly ground black pepper

Preheat the oven to 200°C/400°F/gas mark 6. Soften the shallot and garlic in the goose fat, and make a stuffing by mixing in the chopped herbs, diced ham, the chopped liver of the chicken, the shredded slice of white bread, and the seasoning. Stuff the chicken with this mixture, and arrange the slices of bacon over the chicken breast.

Set the bird on its side, in a tin that just fits it, and roast for about 1¼ hours, basting every 15 minutes, and turning after 20 minutes. Towards the end of the cooking time, put it on its back so that it cooks evenly. If the fat starts to burn, add some water or stock to the pan.

While the chicken is cooking, prepare the vegetables. Remove tough broad bean skins by blanching them then slipping them off. When almost ready to serve, cook the vegetables in boiling salted water, for no more than 5 minutes, so that they retain their flavour and crunch, as well as their colour. Dress with a little butter and keep warm.

Once the chicken is cooked, take it out of the oven, cover with foil and let it stand while you make the sauce. Skim the fat from the cooking juices, and deglaze the pan with a little stock or cooking water from the vegetables, scraping all of the bits off the bottom. Boil for a few minutes to reduce, and season to taste. Arrange the green vegetables around the chicken, and serve with the sauce.

PETIT SALE ET MIQUE

Salt Pork with Herbed Dumpling

The mique, *a dumpling-like alternative to bread, has long been a feature of peasant cooking in Périgord. Unlike English dumplings,* miques *are usually large, and should be divided into portions with two forks, rather than a knife.*

SERVES 8
1kg/2¼lb salt pork (*petit salé*)
4 each carrots, leeks, turnips
1 garlic clove

FOR THE MIQUE
550g/1¼lb strong white flour
25g/¾oz fresh yeast or 1 packet 'easy-blend' yeast
2tbsp warm milk
5 eggs
2tbsp goose fat or oil
100g/3½oz bacon, diced
3tbsp chopped parsley and chives

About three hours before you wish to serve the meal, place the flour in a large bowl, add a large pinch of salt, and dissolve the yeast in warm milk. (If you are using dried yeast, follow instructions on the packet). Pour the yeast into a well in the flour, and leave in a warm place, for 10 minutes.

Beat the eggs, and add to the flour together with the fat and other ingredients. Mix with a wooden spoon, then knead to form a smooth dough. Cover with a cloth, and leave in a warm place for two hours.

Rinse the salt pork, but do not soak, and place in a large pot. Cover with water and a lid, and bring to the boil. Simmer, covered, for 1½ hours, then add vegetables and garlic and cook for 30 minutes. Remove the pork and vegetables from the pot and keep warm while you cook the *mique*. Cool the stock just enough to enable you to skim off the fat.

When the dough has doubled in size, knead again and knock back into a ball. Bring the stock back to the boil, gently slide the *mique* in and cover. Turn it over after 30 minutes, and leave to cook until it floats to the surface; this should take about another 20 minutes. During cooking time, the *mique* will double in size. Remove the *mique* and keep warm.

Immediately before serving, skin and slice the meat and place around the *mique* on a serving plate with the vegetables. Serve with cooking liquid, mustard and pickled gherkins.

FAISAN AUX CEPES ET AUX CHATAIGNES

Pheasant with Ceps and Chestnuts

This recipe is suitable for birds in their first year of life; older ones would need more cooking. By cooking the pheasants upside-down in an enclosed pot, the breasts do not dry out, as often happens when you roast them in the conventional way. Brown-capped mushrooms combined with a few dried ceps make a good substitute for fresh ceps if these are not available, and chestnuts are sometimes available ready peeled and cooked in cans or vacuum-sealed bags, which cuts out the tedious business of removing their skins. (Illustrated right)

SERVES 6
1tbsp goose fat
100g/3½oz salt belly pork or bacon, diced
2 pheasants
2tbsp cognac or armagnac
1 onion, chopped
300g/10½oz fresh ceps
or 300g/10½oz brown cap mushrooms and 25g/¾oz dried ceps (if no fresh ceps are available)
150ml/5fl oz white wine, mixed with equal quantity of water or chicken stock
bouquet garni
12 small onions, about the size of the chestnuts
1tbsp butter
1tsp sugar
250g/8½oz chestnuts, prepared weight
salt and freshly ground black pepper

In a large cast-iron casserole, melt the goose fat, and cook the pork or bacon for a few minutes before putting in the pheasants to brown. Turn them over to colour the skin on all sides, and when nicely browned, pour the warmed brandy over the birds and set alight. Turn the pheasants breast-side down, and put the chopped onion and mushrooms into the pot, packing them around the birds. Pour over white wine and stock or water, add seasoning and bouquet garni, and cover tightly with a lid. Simmer gently for about an hour.

When nearly ready to serve, melt the butter in a saucepan, and cook the small onions for about 10 minutes or until soft. Add the sugar, stir around, then put the chestnuts into the pan with the onions. Cook over moderate heat – stirring constantly but carefully, so as not to break them up – until they are slightly caramelized on the outside.

To serve, take the birds from the casserole, joint them, and keep them warm while you reduce the sauce. This may not be necessary if it has partly evaporated during the cooking. Adjust seasoning, remove the bouquet garni, and, using a slotted spoon, take out the mushrooms. Serve these with the pheasant, chestnuts and onions, and the sauce separately.

ENCHAUD DE PORC PERIGOURDIN

Pot-roasted Pork with Wine, Truffles and Garlic

One of the very best recipes of Périgord, a succulent roast which is equally good hot or cold, enchaud is traditionally made with loin of pork. As an alternative to pork loin, use meat cut from the shoulder blade, which, being streaked with fat, is juicier, though not perhaps to everyone's taste. Either way, the meat should be stripped of skin and most of the outer layer of fat, but not tied by the butcher.

As with many recipes that include truffles as one of the ingredients, this dish is also excellent without them, but special occasions may warrant the extravagance. (Illustrated left)

SERVES 8
1.8kg/4lb pork, cut from the loin or
shoulder blade, boned weight
2 or 3 garlic cloves cut into thin slivers
1 black truffle, fresh or tinned, peeled and
sliced
1tbsp goose fat
150ml/5fl oz dry white wine, mixed with
2 tbsp water

The day before you plan to serve the *enchaud*, lay the meat out, fat side down, on a board, and cut small slits in the flesh at intervals. Place slivers of garlic and truffle, if using, into these slits. Sprinkle with salt and pepper. Roll up the meat with the garlic and truffle on the inside, and tie as neatly as possible with string. If using shoulder, the result will not be as neat, but this is not vital. Set the meat to rest in a cool place for 24 hours.

When ready to start cooking, preheat the oven to 160°C/325°F/gas mark 3. In a large cast-iron casserole, heat the goose fat, then place the rolled pork in the hot fat to brown. Turn over several times, to brown all surfaces. Add wine and water to the pot, cover tightly, and place in the oven. Cook for 2–2½ hours, checking towards the end of the cooking time to make sure that the liquid has not all evaporated, and adjusting as necessary. Leave the covered pot to rest for a few minutes before carving and serving the meat.

FILET DE BOEUF SARLADAIS

Fillet of Beef with Truffles and Foie Gras

Now considered a classic of périgourdin cuisine, this rich and costly dish, in which a fillet of beef is studded with truffles and served with foie gras, has not always been a feature of traditional cookery. Even the wealthy preferred to feast on fat poultry and game; cattle were regarded as beasts of burden, not sources of red meat. It was only when butchers' shops became commonplace that people started to eat red meat regularly, and to invent sumptuous dishes such as this.

SERVES 6–8
1 black truffle
Fillet of beef weighing 1.35–1.8kg/3–4lb
225g/8oz streaky unsmoked bacon
2tbsp brandy or eau-de-vie
1 glass white wine
salt and freshly ground black pepper
2 thin slices baguette per person, to serve
About 100g/3½oz *pâté de foie gras* or *foie*
***gras entier*, to serve**

FOR THE SAUCE PERIGUEUX
4 shallots, finely chopped
1tbsp goose fat
1tbsp plain flour
30g/1oz dried ceps
350ml/12fl oz white wine
2tbsp brandy
5tbsp madeira
300ml/10fl oz rich duck or beef stock
salt and freshly ground black pepper

Preheat the oven to 200°C/400°F/gas mark 6. Cut the truffle in two, and, if using tinned or bottled truffles, save the juice: this will be used to make the sauce. Cut thin matchsticks from half of the truffle, and stick these into the meat at intervals, first making a hole with a cocktail stick or skewer. Wrap the meat with slices of bacon, season with salt and pepper, and set on a rack in a roasting tin. Pour brandy and wine into the tin, and put the meat in to cook. For the cooking time, allow 15 minutes per pound plus an extra 15 minutes. Baste with pan juices several times during cooking.

While the meat is cooking, make the sauce. First soften the shallots in goose fat, stir in flour, then add dried ceps and white wine and simmer over low heat, half-covered, for about 30 minutes. Strain, squeezing out all of the liquid and discarding the solids, then add the brandy, madeira and stock to the liquid. Bring back to the boil, and simmer for 30 minutes. Cut the remaining truffle into tiny dice, and add these to the sauce, together with any juice. Check seasoning and keep warm until ready to serve.

When the meat is cooked, add the cooking juices to the sauce, having first skimmed off any excess fat. Keep the meat warm.

To serve, toast the slices of baguette, spread with foie gras, and place alongside slices of beef fillet and *sauce Périgueux*.

MILLASSOU

Pumpkin and Cornmeal Cake with Raisins

Various versions of millassou *exist, some made with wheat flour, some with the addition of chopped prunes, as well as raisins. In the past, butter would rarely be used in périgourdin farmhouses, and goose fat or oil would have been added in its place. This is a wonderfully comforting cake for autumn, served on its own, still warm from the oven, or surrounded by a pool of* crème anglaise.

SERVES 6–8
2tbsp rum
100g/3½oz raisins
550g/1¼lb pumpkin, peeled and cubed
300ml/10fl oz milk
75g/2½oz butter, plus extra
200g/7oz maize flour
150g/5½oz caster sugar
2tsp vanilla sugar
4 eggs, separated

Warm the rum and put the raisins in it to soak for an hour so that they plump up. Preheat the oven to 200°C/400°F/gas mark 6.

Cook the pumpkin cubes in the milk, then purée together. Stir the butter into the hot liquid until it melts. Mix maize flour, sugar and vanilla sugar into the pumpkin purée.

Lightly whisk the egg yolks, and add them to the pumpkin mixture, tip in raisins and rum, and beat until smooth with a wooden spoon.

In another bowl, whisk the eggs whites until stiff, then fold them carefully into the other ingredients. Butter a 24cm/9½in cake tin, and pour in the cake mixture. Bake for 30–40 minutes, until golden brown on top and cooked through. Allow to cool in the tin before serving.

SOUFFLE GLACE AUX NOIX

Frozen Walnut Mousse

Half-way between a parfait *and a mousse, this delicious frozen dessert is one of the specialities at La Meynardie, near Salignac, where they serve it with* crème anglaise. *(Illustrated above)*

SERVES 6
55g/2oz walnuts
4 eggs, separated
3tbsp eau-de-noix (walnut liqueur)
250ml/8fl oz crème fraîche or whipping cream
125g/4oz icing sugar

In a dry frying pan, toast the walnuts over medium heat, then leave to cool. Chop them finely and set aside.

Beat the egg yolks with half of the sugar until pale and creamy, then add the chopped walnuts and liqueur. Whip the cream and fold gently into the egg yolks and sugar.

In a clean, dry bowl, whisk the egg whites until stiff, then incorporate the remaining

sugar, still whisking. Carefully fold the whisked whites into the egg yolk mixture, pour into ramekin moulds, and freeze for at least 3 hours. They can be kept in the freezer for up to 24 hours before serving, but are best not left much longer.

Serve in the ramekins, or if you prefer, unmould the soufflés and serve on a pool of *crème anglaise.*

PATE DE COINGS

Quince Paste

Quinces have a wonderful perfume. This thick paste is also popular in Spain and Portugal, where it is eaten with cheese, but in Périgord, it is more usual to serve it cut into squares and dusted with sugar, as petit fours *with coffee.*

quinces
sugar

Cut the quinces into quarters, then put in a saucepan with enough water to cover. Bring to the boil, and cook until soft – about 20 minutes. Strain, reserving the juice to make quince jelly. Purée the cooked fruit in a food mill or food processor, then push the pulp through a sieve, discarding cores and skins.

Measure the pulp and for every litre/1¾pt, add 800g/1¾lb of sugar. Dissolve the sugar in the pulp over a gentle heat, then bring to the boil. Simmer until thick, taking care not to get burned by the spitting, bubbling paste.

Oil some shallow dishes or trays, and pour in the paste to a depth of about 2cm/¾in. Leave to set in a dry, warmish place for 2 days, turning over each piece half-way through. Cut into squares, dust with sugar, and store in airtight containers.

TARTE AUX NOIX

Walnut Tart

Walnut tart appears in many guises through-out the Périgord and Quercy. Some versions have a chocolate covering in place of the top layer of pastry; others have a thin glaze of egg white and sugar; this one has a pastry lid. (Illustrated right)

SERVES 6

FOR THE PASTRY

125g/4½oz cold butter
200g/7oz plain flour
55g/2oz caster sugar
30g/1oz ground walnuts
1 egg, beaten

FOR THE FILLING

200g/7oz sugar, flavoured with vanilla
1 generous tbsp crème fraîche
3 eggs, beaten
140g/5oz walnuts, lightly crushed

To make the pastry, first grate the cold butter into the flour, and rub in quickly with your fin-gertips until the mixture resembles fine bread-crumbs. (If using a food processor, take care not to overprocess.) Add sugar and ground walnuts, then mix in the beaten egg, gathering up the mixture in your fingers, and kneading very lightly to form an even dough. It is not necessary to let this type of pastry rest before cooking, but in hot weather, chill it for 30 min-utes or so, to firm it up slightly before rolling.

Preheat the oven to 190°C/375°F/gas mark 5, and place a metal baking sheet inside.

To make the filling, dissolve the sugar in 100ml/3½fl oz warm water, and heat gently to make a syrup. When the sugar is dissolved, bring to the boil, and allow to bubble until the liquid is mid-brown in colour and smells of caramel. Remove from the heat, and beat in the crème fraiche, taking care because it will splut-ter as it enters the hot caramel. If the caramel solidifies when you add the cold cream, put the pan back over gentle heat and stir until it dissolves again. Take off the heat, and keep stirring until the mixture is of even consistency, then leave to cool for about 10 minutes. Mix in the beaten eggs (reserving a little to brush the top of the tart), then add the crushed walnuts.

Divide the pastry into two parts, one slightly larger than the other, and roll out the larger part. Line a greased 20cm/8in loose-bottomed flan tin with the pastry. (It may break apart a bit during this process, but do not worry, as any holes can easily be mended by filling them with spare scraps from the edges.) Pour in the filling, roll out the remaining pastry, and place on top of the tart. Brush with beaten egg. Bake for about 30 minutes, until the pastry is brown. Remove from the oven, and allow to cool before cutting. The tart can be served warm or cold, and is delicious with vanilla ice-cream.

ABOVE *The Benedictine abbey of Brantôme, reputed to have been founded by Charlemagne in 769, on the river Dronne. Rebuilt many times over the centuries, the abbey buildings were deconsecrated in 1791. Set between two branches of the Dronne, Brantôme is an island town, with some fine renaissance houses, and a park with classical pavilions beside the river.*
RIGHT *A market stallholder's umbrella provides a convenient place to keep a lunchtime baguette.*
FAR RIGHT *Slices of pumpkin, for making into millassou, (Pumpkin and Cornmeal Cake, page 38).*

PERIGORD BLANC

Travelling north and west from Sarlat, the transition from Périgord Noir to Périgord Blanc is a gentle one. There is no official boundary, just a gradual change in the landscape and architecture, from scrubby woodland to wide open pastures, from picture-book villages of golden stone to more workaday settlements of white or grey limestone. Still farther north, towards Nontron, white stone gives way to the rendered walls and slate roofs of the Limousin. This region, known as Périgord Vert, is indeed remarkably green, with forests of tall chestnut and oak, watered by copious rainfall. To the west, among the pines of the Double forest, the remains of timber-framed farm buildings lie deserted, superseded by modern bungalows.

Unlike the Périgord Noir, which somehow seems to look back to the past, the northern part of the Dordogne has changed with the times. Though still intensely rural, this is a land where horticulture has turned into agriculture, where thousands of tons of strawberries and apples are grown each year and where new, industrial cheese factories have been built. Even the famous black truffle is virtually extinct in that region, although it is currently enjoying a renaissance in the northern *causses* (limestone uplands) around Sorges and Excideuil.

In the centre of Périgord Blanc, so called because of its chalky white stone, is the ancient city of Périgueux. It was prosperous in Roman times, with its own arena, baths and temples, and later developed around the Byzantine-style cathedral of Saint-Front during the Middle Ages. Today, the narrow cobbled streets around the cathedral hum with life and activity yet the ban on traffic means that the atmosphere is calm. Richly decorated Renaissance houses are a common sight in these alleyways, with elegant doorways and interior courtyards, and there are dozens of top-quality food and clothes shops. Périgueux has moved gracefully into this century – neither forgetting its past, nor being hampered by it.

THE COUNTRY COMES TO TOWN

On Wednesday and Saturday mornings, the Place de la Clautre outside Périgueux's Saint-Front cathedral is alive with the animated buzz of conversation. It is market day and people from the surrounding countryside have come into town; here, beneath brightly coloured umbrellas, they sell their produce and catch up on the latest gossip.

TOP Bottled beans, asparagus, wild mushrooms and fruit, in the store-room at La Chouette Gourmande, a small auberge deep in the countryside near Nontron. The traditional dishes of Périgord are chef-patronne Micheline Dupin's speciality. In the walled vegetable garden, Mme Dupin grows most of the fruit and vegetables for the restaurant, and in summer she gathers elderflowers and rose petals to make fragrant sorbets (see page 66).
ABOVE Purple-tipped asparagus on sale in the market at Périgueux.

Marcel Guinot, a pensioner, comes from Champcevinel, just to the north of Périgueux. He raises pigeons, rabbits and chickens for the table, feeding them only on maize, oats and barley – no industrial animal feed – so they will taste good. He sells the pigeons after two months, when they weigh about 750g/1¾lb, and have lost their down. Too young, and they have no flavour, he says. Fresh peas are in season, and so a *compôte de pigeons* (see page 63) seems a good idea. Further down, Eliane Grossin displays her range of cheeses, made from unpasteurized cows' and goats' milk at the farm in Saint-Crépin d'Auberoche. Before buying, customers are invited to taste a young, fresh cows' milk cheese, and admire the variety of *chèvres* – dozens of different shapes and flavours – as well as home-made fruit yogurts.

The queue for fish in the Poissonerie Moderne spills out on to the pavement, and André Samson, the proprietor, is taking advantage of his captive audience to offer free tastings of freshly boiled *bulots* (whelks), still warm and tasting of pepper and the sea. Meanwhile, live crabs try to make their escape, and an eel slithers across the counter, on its way to join fish such as *rascasse* (used in bouillabaisse). Apart from selling an impressive range of fresh fish, the Poissonerie Moderne also operates as a *traiteur*, and you can buy ready-cooked specialities such as *brandade* (salt cod purée), *anguilles* (eels) *à la persillade* and *quenelles de brochet* (pike). There are treats for the shellfish gourmet, too: *moules marinières* or *mouclade* (mussels in a thickened saffron sauce) and *palourdes roses farcies* (stuffed clams).

Nearby, in the covered market, Les Halles du Coderc, the stallholders specialize in meat and charcuterie. Jean-Pierre Dubreuil proudly advertizes his traditional fare – '*charcuterie naturelle du bon vieux temps*' (traditional charcuterie from natural ingredients); prize-winning *pâté campagnard*, *grillons de confit de porc* (potted meat), *rillettes d'oie* (coarse goose pâté) and *fromage de tête* (brawn) are displayed in huge earthenware bowls, while nestling alongside are *boudins noirs* and *blancs*. Outside, the open-air stalls display ready-trussed chickens, with the gizzards neatly tied on to each bird, bunches of chickens' feet and bowls of bright red blood for making the stuffing, *la farce noire*, or *les sanguettes*, cakes of cooked blood which are diced and fried with garlic and parsley. It is no good being squeamish in this part of the world.

Those with faint-hearted appetites would feel more at home just around the corner, at Marchal & Pautet, an exquisite patisserie and *salon de thé*. Gérard Joly is the master *pâtissier*, and his wife Francine looks after the shop, ushering elegantly clad women and courting couples through to the powder blue tea-room, or handing lollipops to the children of favourite customers. She explains that their real speciality is chocolate, and walnuts, of course, in many glorious combinations. As well as *la tarte aux noix*, with or without chocolate, there are *périgourdins* – ambrosial wedges of light walnut macaroon sandwiched together with whipped walnut cream, and encased in rich, dark chocolate, *truffières*, made with rum-soaked raisins and chocolate mousse, and *tartes aux pommes et au chocolat*, an inspired combination. In addition to what Gérard Joly calls '*la vraie pâtisserie française*', he makes various confections based on the fashionable *bavarois*, a smooth mousse-like cake with a thin sponge base, including a highly successful copy of Gaston Lenôtre's celebrated chocolate creation *Opéra*, which they call the *Triomphe*. But it seems that tastes are changing, and customers are once again asking for the old favourites such as *gâteau praliné* and *tarte aux fruits*, so, much to Gérard Joly's satisfaction, he can go back to being a real pastry-cook.

CONFIT DE CANARD

Submerged in its own fat and thus sealed from the air, confit *of duck (above) or goose was originally devised as a method of preserving meat before the days of refrigeration. It is the ultimate convenience food, as the preserved duck can be quickly grilled or sautéd before serving, making the skin beautifully crisp.*

To make confit *at home, take 4 duck legs, with the thigh attached, and rub them with sea salt. For every 450g/1lb weight of duck, use 15g/½oz of salt. Leave in a cool place for 24 hours. The next day, brush off the salt, and melt a little duck or goose fat in a large saucepan. Fry the duck legs, skin side down, so that the fat runs from the skin. Add a bay leaf and about 1kg/2¼lb of goose or duck fat, enough to cover the meat, and allow to melt. Season with black pepper and simmer very gently, uncovered, for 2 hours. Allow the duck to cool in the fat for an hour, then transfer to a sterilized jar. Pour melted fat over to cover the pieces of meat, seal and store in the refrigerator until needed. It will keep for a month, and improve in flavour.*

Périgueux market, outside the cathedral of Saint-Front, with (left) some of the produce on sale.

LEFT A tranquil scene by the banks of the river Isle, where the natural force of the water is harnessed to power the three waterwheels of the walnut mill at Rochevideau.
BELOW The pepperpot towers of le Château de Hautefort, birthplace of the author Eugène Le Roy, who wrote a series of historical novels set in Périgord. His best known work is the story of Jacquou le Croquant, *published in 1899 and recently dramatized for television.*

THE WALNUT MILL, ROCHEVIDEAU

At Rochevideau, near Brantôme, the Debord family start making walnut oil in late October, once the nuts have had time to dry out, and continue until the end of March. The ancient mill (above) is driven by water power, and makes a wonderful, rhythmic grinding noise as it turns. As you enter, the interior seems to be in near darkness, but gradually shapes separate themselves from the gloom – a huge granite millstone that crushes the nuts to a paste, and the cast-iron pan, or poêle, *in which the paste is heated. An enormous press, where the oil is extracted through thick cotton pads, stands near the door, and beside it, the vat where the oil is stored. It takes about 5kg/11lb of unshelled walnuts, or 2kg/4½lb of kernels, to make 1l/1¾pt of oil.*

You can buy the freshly pressed oil direct from the mill. If you have forgotten to bring a container, the oil is ladled into recycled Perrier bottles, then wrapped in newspaper. Kept in a cool, dark place, it will stay fresh for at least a year. As well as walnut oil, Marcel Debord makes hazelnut oil, which he likes to pour over a plate of warm haricot beans. It can also be used to add extra flavour and richness to hazelnut cakes and pastries.

LA BONNE CUISINE DU PERIGORD

It was Andrée Maze, better known as La Mazille, who, early this century, first exploded the widespread notion that everybody in Périgord lived on foie gras and truffles. She was not a native of the region (she was born in Paris, where her father was an engineer), but she spent each summer with the rest of her family in the sleepy village of Planèze, in the Isle valley not far from Périgueux, and there she learned to appreciate *La Bonne Cuisine du Périgord*, which was to be the title of the book she published in 1929. It became a classic, and is still in print.

'Maybe one eats a little more than elsewhere,' she writes in the introduction, 'but above all, one eats better, and that is due to the skill of the cooks.' She explains that not only do they have at their disposal the very best ingredients – and here she means such everyday food as chicken, onions, garlic, beans and tomatoes, as well as foie gras and truffles – but they also seem to have an instinctive knowledge of what best to do with them. Several of the recipes in the book are attributed to Victorine, an old and loyal family servant and a native of Périgord, whose cooking skills and extensive knowledge of traditional cuisine obviously inspired La Mazille. The result was a work of lasting significance, which has been a source of inspiration and reference for many who followed her.

PRICKLY CUSTOMERS

Chestnuts, once a staple food in the northern fringes of Périgord, form an integral part of the folklore of regional cooking. Their importance has declined dramatically, however, and they seldom appear on restaurant menus today, perhaps due to their past history as peasants' food and their association with poverty, or to the time-consuming business of peeling them.

An old local recipe for *les châtaignes blanchies* describes a midday meal of steamed chestnuts and soup. Once the outer skins had been peeled, a special tool called a *déboiradour* or a *ruffadou*, which resembles a large pair of wooden pinking shears, was used to rub off the inner skins. The chestnuts were then steamed in a lidded pot, either wrapped in cabbage leaves or placed on a bed of potatoes, and tipped out, steaming hot, on to a cloth spread on the kitchen table, for everyone to help themselves.

In the past, the chestnut forests were carefully maintained, the trees pruned and fertilized, and the undergrowth cleared. Dead leaves were collected and used as bedding for cattle, and the chestnuts provided the basis of the peasants' diet. In *Jacquou le Croquant*, Eugène Le Roy's popular novel set among the poor in nineteenth-century Périgord, the hero describes a typical meal of soup and chestnuts, adding 'they are good, steamed chestnuts, when they are fresh, but when they have been through the dryer, they are not the same thing at all.' In order to preserve the crop for as long as possible, chestnuts were often placed above a smouldering fire in a special outhouse to dry, and must have tasted very smoky.

In autumn the *charcutiers* of Thiviers, Saint-Pardoux-La-Rivière and Mialet all make a local speciality, *boudins aux châtaignes* (black pudding stuffed with chestnuts), which are sliced and fried, and served with sautéed apples, potato purée or salad.

CHESTNUTS

In French there are two words for sweet chestnuts: les châtaignes *and* les marrons. *The tree, however, is always called a* châtaignier, *not to be confused with the horse chestnut,* le marronnier d'Inde. *The* marron *is a bigger, single fruit than the segmented* châtaigne, *and it is much easier to peel, so it has more commercial importance.*

In the past, chestnuts formed an important part of the peasants' diet, having a high calorific value, and being easy to cultivate in the damp climate of northern Périgord. By soaking them in cold water for a week, or by drying them over a fire, they can be preserved for many months, although they taste much better fresh. Chestnuts are used for making jam, liqueurs and sweets, but these food products pale into insignificance today compared with the exploitation of the tree for its timber and for the ceps which grow beneath it. More often than not, the chestnuts are left lying on the ground to rot, while people hunt furiously for the elusive cep. This is a shame as chestnuts are very versatile: their starchy sweetness adds both flavour and texture to savoury soups, stews and stuffings for poultry, and also combines particularly well with chocolate, as in Chestnut and Chocolate Mousse (see page 64).

GASTRONOMY
A LA TRAPPE

*Once the haunt of wolves and bandits, the forest
of the Double, south of Ribérac, remains one
of the least populated regions of Périgord.
Here, in this unlikely spot, a gastronomic
delight – Trappist cheese – is produced by the
nuns of the abbey of Notre Dame de Bonne
Espérance at Echourgnac.
In 1868, a group of Trappist monks founded
the abbey to help the disease-ridden people of
the Double to wipe out malaria, and to make a
living from raising dairy cattle. They came
from Port-du-Salut, and with their cheese-
making experience were able to set up a
fromagerie to provide the peasants with a
ready-made market for their milk. The cheese
bore a striking resemblance to Port Salut, with
its mild flavour and soft, creamy texture. In 1923,
the monks were replaced by nuns, who still
make the cheese, La Trappe Echourgnac.
Recently, they have introduced another, richer
cheese, Saint-Heblon, with a mould-ripened
crust and a more pronounced flavour. Both
cheeses are matured in vaulted chambers
within the abbey, La Trappe Echourgnac for
three weeks, Saint-Heblon for two.*

BLACK DIAMONDS

Until the outbreak of phylloxera in the 1870s, vines were grown on the poor, chalky soils of north-eastern Périgord, around Thiviers, Sorges and Excideuil. Although the wine produced there was not of the highest quality, the destruction wrought by the dreaded disease was initially seen as a disaster for the *vignerons*, but it was to turn to their advantage eventually.

The very same soils had always been known to encourage the growth of a mysterious black fungus, *Tuber melanosporum*, the famous black truffle of Périgord. The truffle had long been regarded as a gift from God, but in the 1830s a certain M. Montagnac of Sorges conceived the idea of encouraging the growth of truffles by planting *truffières*, or truffle oaks produced from acorns harvested from trees where truffles had already been found. Ten years later, he was harvesting small quantities of truffles from the two-hectare plot, which were later to rise to yields of some 200 kilograms. Further trials showed that, although the fungus cannot be cultivated in a predictable way like other crops, its growth could certainly be encouraged – a development of real commercial significance.

It was only after phylloxera had destroyed the vineyards, however, that the idea really took off. Soon the farmers were planting *truffières* on a massive scale, in the hope that within ten or 15 years they would be harvesting plenty of 'black diamonds' that would more than compensate for the loss of the vines. By and large they were successful, and production reached its peak at the turn of the century. It started to decrease with the onset of war, and has since dropped continuously to the relatively small amount that is harvested today.

This trend may be about to take a turn for the better, however, as the efforts of *trufficulteurs* such as Jean Clergerie are rewarded. In 1972, he started to plant truffle oaks on his land, a farm in Saint-Panthaly-d'Excideuil, chiefly devoted to apple production. By forming the Groupement des Trufficulteurs de Saint-Panthaly d'Excideuil with a number of local farmers, he was able to share his experiences with others and enlist expert advice from the Chamber of Agriculture. Already the results are encouraging, with a harvest of 250 kilograms/550lb between them in 1991, and even more since then.

Walking through a truffle plantation, it is hard to believe that anything is thriving there. The trees – oaks and hazelnuts – are stunted and covered with lichen, and the stony ground around many of the trees is bare, denuded even of weeds. In fact, this scorched effect – known as *brûlé* – is the sign that truffles are likely to be growing underground.

Not all of the trees produce truffles, but in Jean Clergerie's experience about half have done so, and much sooner than he had expected. The ground must be cleared of weeds in April, when the mycelium is dormant and there is no danger of damaging its fragile filaments. Apart from irrigating in dry years, there is nothing left to do but watch and wait until December, when the harvest can begin. After that, he goes out every week with the dog and expects to get a few kilograms each time, which he sells at the market at Excideuil. His largest truffle weighed 250g/8½oz, and was about the size of a golf ball, but that one never made it to market – he ate it. At prices which hover around 3000 Francs a kilogram, it was quite a find, but for Jean Clergerie the rewards of trufficulture are quite clearly not merely financial. For him, it is a passion, a revival of a local tradition that was in danger of extinction.

*LEFT Truffle-grower Jean Clergerie, with
his dog Diane, which has been specially trained
to detect the presence of truffles beneath
the ground, using her keen sense of smell.
With every successful find, she gets a
biscuit as a reward.
RIGHT A country lane near Sainte-Foy-de-Longas.
BELOW Cereal crops, interspersed with patches
of scrubby woodland, dominate
the landscape in Périgord Blanc.
Isolated farmsteads stand out from the
background of maize, wheat and sunflowers.*

Summer truffles, *Tuber aestivum*, do not cause the tell-tale *brûlé* of the vegetation, and are found beneath tall, healthy oaks on a neighbouring patch of ground. Jean Clergerie likens the aroma of the summer truffle to *vin ordinaire*, while the winter variety is the Saint-Emilion of truffles. It was only after training a dog that Jean Clergerie has been able to harvest summer truffles, because of the difficulty of locating them without the clue of the patch of *brûlé*. (In the past, pigs were trained to sniff out truffles, but today, dogs are considered to be less trouble.) Another commonly used method of finding truffles involves observing the movements of a certain kind of fly, but it is only useful on bare ground, and therefore reserved for the harvest of winter truffles.

Jean Clergerie and his group of *trufficulteurs*, together with another local truffle expert, Jean Rebière, helped to set up the Ecomusée de la Truffe in Sorges in 1982. The museum contains a wealth of information about the history, geography, botany, gastronomy and folklore of truffles and even has its own truffle plantation nearby, where you can see the trees and associated flora in context. The village of Sorges also has an excellent restaurant, L'Auberge de la Truffe, where, not surprisingly, you can sample the fabled fungus.

THE ART OF APPLE GROWING

Apples grow well in the cool, damp climate of north-eastern Périgord, and farmers have always had a few trees dotted here and there to provide for their own needs. Some of them even make cider, although not on a commercial scale, and generally it is only sold at the farm gate, if at all.

In recent years, however, vast orchards of Golden Delicious, American Red, Jonagold and Granny Smith have appeared on the hillsides, serried rows of neatly trimmed trees stretching

RIGHT Micheline Dupin, at work in the kitchen garden at La Chouette Gourmande, her country hotel and restaurant, at Saint-Front sur Nizonne. Like many other gardeners in Périgord (above, top and far right) she bottles surplus fruit and vegetables for the store-cupboard.

away as far as the eye can see, some of them covered with white netting to protect them from hail damage. The department of Dordogne now produces a total of 80,000 tonnes of apples each year, mainly on these northern slopes. Favoured for their keeping qualities, heavy cropping and regular shape and size, these apple varieties have become the favourites of European supermarkets, where they fill the shelves in gleaming uniformity.

Happily, one or two small growers prefer the old French varieties, such as Reinette Grise, which, as well as having a fine flavour, are well adapted to the climate so need less treatment against disease. Jean-Claude Jarry is one such grower, and since he uses no artificial fertilizers or chemical sprays at all at his farm in Mialet, he can market his produce under the *Nature et Progrès* label. As well as apples, he sells home-made apple juice, with no additives or preservatives, and a blend of apple and raspberry juice. Farther north, Philippe François makes cider and apple, pear and grape juice, which he sells direct from the farm in Firbeix and at local markets.

A FARMHOUSE WELCOME

At a time when small farmers are finding it increasingly difficult to survive, the concept of agro-tourism plays an increasingly important part in the rural economy, and it was in the department of Dordogne that the *ferme-auberge* was born. Now there are over 80 farms listed in '*Bienvenue à la Ferme en Périgord*', an annual booklet with details of farms that offer meals, rooms or camping facilities, or that sell produce direct to the public (see page 147).

There are strict rules governing the running of a *ferme-auberge* to ensure that the food is not only home-cooked, but that most of the ingredients are produced on the farm, and that the menu is composed of regional dishes. The dining-room must be decorated in local rustic

ABOVE AND LEFT The Double forest, though dank and gloomy in winter, is a paradise for hunters and fishermen, who are usually out in force on Sunday mornings. During the season, they can be seen in forest clearings or on the banks of the river, guns or fishing-rods at the ready, dogs at their heels. Deer and wild boar are the most prized trophies, with pheasant, partridge, hare and rabbit the quarry for small game hunters. Sadly, genuinely wild game is becoming very rare, and is supplemented with creatures which are raised in captivity, and then released for la chasse. At the end of the season, the hunters gather in the village hall for a celebratory feast of marcassin (roast young wild boar) or civet de chevreuil (Venison Casserole, see page 62).

TOP *Plastic tunnels are used to extend the strawberry season, from early spring to late autumn.*

ABOVE *As recently as 1970, the growing of strawberries was of little commercial significance in the Dordogne region, but today the department produces more than any other in France, with a crop of some 25,000 metric tons each year. Cultivation is at its most intensive around Vergt, where the fruit is sold by auction twice a day during the season.*

style, and seat no more than 60 people. Inevitably, a menu composed of regional specialities often has a repetitive ring, and *pâté de foie gras* followed by *confit de canard*, though delicious, can seem just a mite too rich on the third night in succession. To avoid this, it is worth telephoning ahead when planning to eat in a *ferme-auberge*, in order to discuss the menu. With advance warning, most cooks seem happy to prepare a meal of authentic local dishes that will surprise and delight, and at prices that are sometimes unbelievably low.

La Petite Auberge, at Castagnol near Vergt, is a family venture that currently concentrates on growing strawberries, courgettes and tomatoes, and raising poultry. The farm is largely the responsibility of André Gay, whose parents previously raised cows, sheep, pigs and chickens on the land. The *ferme-auberge* opened in 1989 and is run jointly by his wife Claude and daughter Laurence, who is a talented cook. In winter, guests eat by the open fire in the dining-room; in summer, tables are put out in the flower-filled courtyard.

In autumn, the menu might be as follows. After an aperitif, a thick and tasty *soupe paysanne*, made with potatoes, carrots and haricot beans. Then a *salade composée* of home-grown lettuce, duck breast ham, crisp cubes of bacon, lightly fried slices of apple, croutons and fresh walnuts. For the main course, roast chicken stuffed with wild *trompettes de la mort* (horn of plenty) mushrooms, served with glazed chestnuts and a gratin of courgettes. Local goats' cheeses and *tarte amandine aux pommes* bring the meal to an end. The experience is made even more satisfying by the knowledge that almost every ingredient has been grown or produced on the farm, including the very drinkable *vin ordinaire*.

STRAWBERRY FIELDS

The gradual transition from raising animals to growing strawberries that has taken place on the Gays' farm over the past 20 years is typical of the area. Strawberries are grown on a massive scale in the Dordogne, now the leading producer in France. The fields are concentrated in the area around Vergt, where, during the season, there are two computerized auctions a day devoted solely to the sale of strawberries. From vast refrigerated warehouses just outside the town, the fruit is dispatched all over Europe, mainly to England and Germany. Strawberries are very difficult to grow without recourse to chemical fungicides and pesticides, as they are subject to many viruses, but they are always in demand, and are reasonably profitable for the farmer.

André Gay has three hectares of strawberries, of which 80 per cent grow under plastic tunnels. The harvest starts in April, when the first Gariguette strawberries are ripe, and continues with Elsanta, a Dutch variety that is ready in June, followed by La Selva and an American variety called Fern, both of which fruit from July to October. Another popular variety is La Mara des Bois, which produces smaller fruit with a scent and flavour reminiscent of wild strawberries; of the other varieties, Gariguette has the best flavour.

As strawberries are a recent introduction, they have no place in the traditional cooking of the region, but nowadays *tarte aux fraises* (see page 64) is a favourite treat for Sunday lunch, and always looks irresistible as part of a patissier's window display.

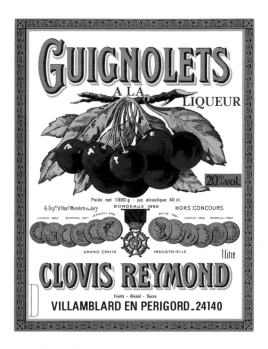

CLOVIS REYMOND

Outside the old distillery in the small town of Villamblard hangs an eye-catching sign: it shows the founder of the family firm, Clovis Reymond, dressed in top hat and tails and clutching a ladle, rising phoenix-like from a cauldron of fiery punch.

Clovis Reymond make a range of nut and fruit aperitifs, eaux-de-vie, liqueurs and fruits in liqueurs, mostly from local fruits. As well as vin de noix, *made from walnuts, they produce* guignolet, *a cherry aperitif, and drinks such as* crème de poire, *which are delicious mixed with white wine as an alternative to Kir.*

They still use methods that have remained virtually unchanged since 1834. In one corner of the old distillery, three magnificent stills of burnished copper rest on a brick plinth, their curved tops capped by graceful swan-necked pipes that plunge into an old condenser.

LE MOULIN DE L'ABBAYE

BRANTOME, TEL 53 05 80 22

In the summer of 1978, Régis and Cathy Bulot discovered an abandoned seventeenth-century mill on the banks of the river Dronne in Brantôme, facing the medieval abbey and the Jardin des Moines. They decided to turn it into a romantic hotel, with a restaurant and terrace by the water's edge.

Today, Le Moulin de l'Abbaye, part of the Relais & Châteaux group, is one of the finest hotels in the region, with a stylish, sunny dining-room, friendly and efficient service and excellent food. Chef Christian Ravinel has reigned in the kitchen almost since the hotel opened. A master of modern cooking, he composes dishes based on the very best of local produce with a unusual lightness of touch. He is a native of Lyons but admits that Périgord is exceptionally rich in good ingredients – foie gras and truffles, of course, but many other treasures, too: walnut oil, verjuice, farm-raised poultry and goats' cheese – and he uses these to create a constantly changing repertoire of inventive new dishes.

CHEVRE FRAIS A LA CREME D'HERBES FRAICHES ET AU JUS DE CELERI

Goats' Cheese with Fresh Herb and Celery Juice Sauce

Christian Ravinel favours local produce in his cooking, and small rounds of fresh goats' cheese are a regional speciality. Chèvre frais has a delicate flavour with none of the pungency of mature goats' cheese, and combines well with celery. This dish is usually served as a starter, but would be equally good as the cheese course. (Illustrated left)

SERVES 8

**6 fresh goats' cheeses, each weighing
approximately 150g/5½oz
fresh herbs, finely chopped
100ml/3½fl oz whipped cream
100g/3½oz chopped walnuts
2 sticks celery, with leaves
3tbsp walnut oil
4tsp white wine vinegar
salt and freshly ground black pepper**

Line the bottom of a terrine with greaseproof paper. Mash 2 of the cheeses together with a fork, and spread evenly over the base of the terrine. Mix the chopped herbs with the whipped cream and the walnuts, and season with salt and pepper to taste. Spread a layer, about 1cm/½in thick, of this cream over the cheese in the terrine. Mash another 2 cheeses together, spread with cream in the same way, then finish with the remaining 2 cheeses. Refrigerate for several hours.

Cut the leaves off the celery, blanch them in boiling water, plunge into cold water to refresh, and mix with a little water in a blender, to make a kind of juice. Strain the juice to remove fibres. Cut the celery into matchsticks. Make a vinaigrette with the walnut oil and vinegar, and season with salt and pepper.

When ready to serve, unmould the terrine and carefully slice it, preferably with an electric carving knife as it is difficult to cut without breaking. Place a slice on each plate, grind some black pepper over, and sprinkle with celery juice and vinaigrette. Garnish with celery matchsticks and serve with walnut bread.

SANDRE A L'EMULSION D'HUILE DE NOIX ET AU VERJUS

Zander with a Sauce of Walnut Oil and Verjuice

Zander, or pike-perch, is a freshwater fish, with white, flaky flesh and a delicate flavour. A native of the rivers of Central Europe, it is caught wild in the Dordogne, and also farmed. Christian Ravinel serves it with a sauce of walnut oil and verjuice (the unfermented juice of sour grapes; see page 105). (Illustrated right)

SERVES 8

**1 zander, weighing about 1.5kg/3½lb,
cleaned
200ml/7fl oz walnut oil
1l/1¾pt verjuice (see page 105)
200ml/7fl oz fish stock
200g/7oz young broad beans, shelled
200g/7oz peas, shelled
55g/2oz butter
55g/2oz chopped walnuts, toasted**

Fillet the fish and divide it up into 8 equal portions. Marinate the fish overnight in 2 tablespoons of walnut oil mixed with 2 tablespoons of verjuice.

Reduce the remaining verjuice to 200ml/7fl oz by simmering in an open pan. Add the fish stock, and whisk in the remaining walnut oil to make a light, frothy sauce.

Cook the broad beans and peas in salted water and drain.

Pan-fry the fish fillets in butter, so that the skin is well browned. Divide the beans and peas between 8 dinner plates, place a fish fillet on each, top with walnuts, and pour over the sauce. Serve immediately.

LE LION D'OR

MANZAC-SUR-VERN, TEL 53 54 28 09

In a quiet backwater of Périgord, the village of Manzac-sur-Vern has no tourist attractions, sights or curiosities – only a belltower, a garage and a few shops. So Jean-Paul and Nelly Beauvais, owners of the Hôtel du Lion d'Or, have to attract customers by feeding them well, at no-nonsense prices. And in this they are successful, because people come back time and time again, from Mussidan, Périgueux, Saint-Astier and even from England.

Born and brought up in Manzac, Jean-Paul Beauvais took over the running of the family hotel in 1983, having trained as a chef in Grenoble and returned to his native village with his wife Nelly, who comes from Normandy. Very soon his inventive ideas for preparing local produce became known in the area, and customers began to flock to the restaurant.

FEUILLETE DE MOULES AU SAFRAN

Mussels in a Saffron Sauce with Flaky Pastry

Jean-Paul Beauvais buys fish and shellfish from the Poissonerie Moderne in Périgueux, where the produce is always sparklingly fresh and of top quality. He manages to keep prices down by using relatively inexpensive ingredients in an imaginative way, and this starter is one of the dishes that keeps customers coming back for more. (Illustrated left)

SERVES 4
4 rectangles of puff pastry, each 8 x 12cm/
3 x 5in
1kg/2¼lb live mussels
55g/2oz shallots, chopped
4tbsp white wine
200ml/7fl oz fish broth
10 strands of saffron
100ml/3½fl oz crème fraîche
25g/¾oz butter
100g/3½oz leeks, trimmed and cut into
julienne strips about 2.5 cm/1in long
2 tomatoes, peeled, deseeded and diced
1tbsp chopped fresh chives

Preheat the oven to 200°C/400°F/gas mark 6. Lay the pastry rectangles on a greased baking sheet, and bake for 20–25 minutes, until golden brown and puffed up. Keep warm.

Prepare the mussels, scrubbing to remove any sand or dirt, and pulling away any beard. Discard any that are broken or open. Soften the shallots with the white wine, in a lidded pan large enough to hold all the mussels, over gentle heat for 5 minutes. Add the mussels, cover tightly, and allow to steam until the shells have opened, about 5 minutes.

Strain, retaining the cooking liquid. Remove mussels from their shells, discarding any that have not opened, and keep warm. Strain the cooking liquid through a fine sieve, and mix half of it with the fish broth. Heat gently, add the saffron and crème fraîche, and simmer, uncovered, over low heat.

Melt the butter, add leek strips, and cook gently until soft but still retaining their colour.

Split the pastry rectangles in half horizontally, and lay the bottom halves on plates. Strew with leek strips and mussels, leaving some over to decorate the finished dish. Pour over some of the sauce, and place pastry lids on top. Surround the feuilletés with more sauce, mussels, and the diced tomatoes, and decorate with chopped chives. Serve immediately.

TARTE TATIN AUX BRUGNONS

Nectarine Upside-down Tart

Tarte Tatin is a speciality of the Loire, but at Le Lion d'Or this famous apple tart has been adapted to the nectarine. (Illustrated right)

SERVES 4
4tbsp sugar for caramel
4 ripe nectarines, sliced
4 circular sheets of puff pastry, each about 13cm/15in in diameter

FOR THE APRICOT COULIS
butter, for greasing
100g/3½oz sugar
sprig of fresh mint
225g/8oz apricots, stones removed

Preheat the oven to 220°C/425°F/gas mark 7. Put 4 tablespoons of sugar in a small saucepan, and cover with just enough water to dissolve the sugar. Heat gently, and boil the syrup, tipping and turning the pan so that it browns evenly. Take off the heat, and put the pan into a bowl of cold water to stop the caramel cooking. Butter four 11cm/4in tartlet tins, and pour caramel over the base of each, dividing it evenly. Arrange nectarine slices over the caramel, overlapping in a circle. Cover each with puff pastry, and bake for 15–20 minutes.

While the tarts are cooking, prepare the apricot coulis: make a syrup with the remaining sugar and mint leaves (reserving some for decoration), then add the apricots. Bring to the boil, simmer until cooked, remove mint leaves, and purée apricots and syrup in the electric blender.

When ready to serve, pour some apricot sauce on each plate, place the tarts, upside-down, on top, and decorate with mint leaves.

TOURAIN BLANCHI

White Garlic Soup

One of the classics of périgourdin cooking, this delicate, creamy soup requires hardly any ingredients, and can be made very easily in next to no time. This version simply uses water, but chicken stock can be used instead for a more pronounced flavour.

SERVES 2–3
1tbsp goose or duck fat
4 fat garlic cloves, finely sliced
1tbsp flour
1 egg, separated
1tbsp white wine vinegar
salt and freshly ground black pepper
stale bread, to serve (optional)

Melt the goose fat in a large saucepan, and over a low heat, gently soften the garlic in the fat, taking care not to let it burn. While it is cooking, boil some water.

When the garlic is soft, stir the flour into the fat, cook for another 2 minutes over gentle heat, then pour on 500ml (16fl oz) boiling water, stirring constantly so that lumps do not form. Blend well, and simmer for 10 minutes. Season with salt and pepper.

Place the yolk in a basin large enough to hold the soup. Mix the vinegar into the egg yolk. Pour the hot soup on to the egg yolk and vinegar, whisking as you do so, so that the yolk cooks in the hot soup and thickens it at the same time. Quickly whisk in the egg white, so that it, too, cooks in the hot soup, forming white strands as it does so. Season with salt and pepper, and pour the soup into a tureen, where you have placed slices of stale bread. The stale bread is optional; if you prefer, serve it with fresh, crusty bread alongside.

SOUPE AUX CHATAIGNES

Chestnut Soup

Laurence Gay is the talented cook at the family-run ferme-auberge in the hamlet of Castagnol, near Vergt. The name Castagnol refers to the abundance of chesnut trees in the area, and in autumn, the family gather the nuts to make this warming soup.

SERVES 6–8
1 kg/2¼lb chestnuts
55g/2oz butter
whites of 4 leeks, chopped and thoroughly washed
4 carrots, peeled and chopped
2 turnips, peeled and chopped
1 potato, peeled and chopped
3tbsp crème fraîche
salt and freshly ground black pepper

Score the chestnuts' outer skins with a knife, and put in a large pan. Cover with water, and bring to the boil. Simmer for about 10 minutes. Drain a few at a time, and peel both skins, inner and outer, while the chestnuts are still hot. If they start to cool, reheat them in the water, as they are very difficult to peel when cold. Rather than peeling the chestnuts, it is sometimes easier and less time-consuming to cut each in half when cooked, and to scoop out the flesh with a teaspoon.

Melt the butter in a large saucepan with a lid, and throw in the chopped leeks. Sweat gently for 10 minutes, then add the other vegetables and the chestnuts. Season with salt and pepper. Add 2l/3½pt water, cover and bring to the boil. Simmer gently for 45 minutes, then purée in a blender or food mill. Check seasoning, stir in the crème fraîche, and serve.

FOIE GRAS DE CANARD AU CRACQUOU

Pan-Fried Duck's Liver with Flaky Pastry

Maryse Baudrier is an inspired cook, who adapts and invents recipes while always keeping local traditions in mind. At her barn-restaurant, La Grange, deep in the countryside near Jumilhac, you can sit outside on a summer's evening, as the sun goes down over the distant castle. Maryse Baudrier serves a variety of classic périgourdin dishes – poulet au verjus, mique au petit salé, civet de lapin – as well as her own creations, and begins each meal with fragrant home-made aperitifs such as dandelion wine or prugnolier, made from infusing the leaves of the wild sloe in alcohol.

Fresh duck liver is served in many a local restaurant, but this crisp pastry accompaniment – christened 'cracquou' – is Maryse Baudrier's idea. She buys her flour from the miller at Sarrazac, some 10 kilometres away, who supplies her with a special blend for making this appetizing starter.

SERVES 4
1 fresh raw duck foie gras
300ml/½pt sweet Malaga wine (or Sauternes, or Monbazillac)
50g/2oz cold butter, cut into small cubes
salt and freshly ground black pepper

FOR THE CRACQUOU
1kg/2¼lb flour
250g/8½oz rendered pork fat or lard, cut into small pieces
250g/8½oz butter, at room temperature
salt

To make the *cracqou*, put the flour and a large pinch of salt in a large mixing bowl, and add the pork fat. Rub the fat into the flour with your fingertips. Pour in 250ml/8fl oz water, and mix rapidly to form a soft, slightly sticky dough. Do not over-knead. Leave the dough to rest in a cool place for 1 hour.

Roll the dough out to a rectangle about 1–1.5cm/½–¾in. Dot the surface with pieces of the butter, which should be roughly of the same consistency as the dough. Fold the rectangle of dough in three, like a business letter, so that it forms a smaller, narrow rectangle. Roll out, and repeat the folding process. Leave to rest for 30 minutes in a cool place, then repeat the folding and rolling. Do this 3 times, leaving the dough to rest between each rolling and folding.

Preheat the oven to 230°C/450°F/gas mark 8. To cook, first roll out the pastry to about 0.5cm/¼in thickness, and cut into whatever size and shape you require. (Extra pastry can be frozen.) Place on a greased baking sheet, and bake in a hot oven for 10 minutes. The cooked *cracquou* can be allowed to cool, and gently reheated when required.

To prepare the liver, first check that it is clean and free from veins and gristle. With a very sharp knife, cut it carefully into slices about 1cm/½in thick, and season the slices with salt and pepper. Heat a non-stick frying pan and cook the foie gras for 1 minute on each side, or until it feels slightly soft when you press the top with your finger. Do not add any fat; the liver has enough of its own.

Place the foie gras on serving plates, and keep warm while you make the sauce. Pour off any excess fat from the pan and add the wine. Bring the liquid to the boil, and simmer until it has reduced by half. Whisk in the cold butter, check seasoning, pour over the foie gras and serve with the *cracquou* at one side.

ARTICHAUTS AUX ŒUFS DE VILLAMBLARD

Young Artichokes with Walnut Oil and Eggs

When globe artichokes are still young and tender you can eat the whole head, rather than just the heart, or fond. Here, they are cooked in walnut oil and baked in the oven with eggs – perfect for a starter or light lunch dish. (Illustrated above)

SERVES 6 (AS A STARTER)
8 baby artichokes
2tbsp seasoned flour
3tbsp walnut oil
6 eggs
salt and freshly ground black pepper
butter, for greasing

Break off the stems about 5cm/2in from the base of each artichoke, and strip off any tough outer fibres with a sharp knife. Slice off the pointed tips of the leaves at the top of each artichoke, and trim off the lower leaves by the stem, as these are always tough. With a very sharp knife, cut the artichokes vertically into thin slices. Dust with seasoned flour.

Heat the walnut oil in a frying pan, and fry the artichoke slices until golden brown, turning once and covering the pan after they have been turned. They should be cooked after about 10 minutes. Grease a shallow gratin dish, and place the artichoke slices in the dish.

Beat the eggs, and season as for an omelette. Pour them over the artichokes. Bake in the oven for 7–8 minutes, until the eggs have puffed up and are cooked around the outside, but still soft in the middle. Serve hot.

GALETTES DE POMMES DE TERRE A LA TRAPPE

Straw Potato Cakes with Trappist Cheese

The Trappist cheese (see page 46) used in this recipe has a creamy consistency and good melting qualities. It is made in the heart of the Forest of the Double by the Trappist sisters of the Abbey of Notre Dame de Bonne Espérance at Echourgnac. (Illustrated left)

SERVES 4–6
550g/1¼lb floury potatoes
115g/4oz smoked streaky bacon, diced (optional)
115g/4oz Trappist cheese or Port Salut, grated
2 garlic cloves, finely chopped
1 egg, beaten
plain flour
2tbsp goose fat or oil
salt and freshly ground black pepper

Peel and grate the potatoes, then, using a clean tea-towel, pat as much moisture out of them as possible. If using bacon, cook it and add it to the potatoes. Stir the grated cheese, garlic, egg and seasoning into the potatoes. Cover a dinner plate with a layer of flour.

Lift out portions of the potato mixture one at a time, firming each into a patty with your hand before placing on the flour, and coating on both sides. Shake off any excess flour.

Heat the fat in a heavy-based frying pan, then put in the potato cakes. There should be enough to make 8 small cakes, so you may have to cook 2 batches. When the under-sides are brown and crisp, turn the cakes over and lower the heat. Cook for about 20 minutes, turning several times, and serve.

HARICOTS BLANCS A L'HUILE DE NOISETTE

Dried Haricot Beans with Hazelnut Oil

In late summer and early autumn, shrivelled pods containing white haricot beans appear on market stalls. When fresh, they need only gentle simmering for 30 minutes, but the dried beans used as a staple food in winter require soaking and longer cooking. Although they keep well, all pulses are best consumed within a year. In France, buy lingot *beans or those labelled* Coco *or* Soissons; *in Britain use cannellini beans. Walnut oil may be used instead of hazelnut oil.*

SERVES 4–6
225g/8oz dried white beans
sprig of thyme
bay leaf
2 garlic cloves
1 onion, sliced lengthwise
about 2tbsp hazelnut oil
1tbsp chopped parsley
salt and freshly ground black pepper

Bring a pot of water to the boil, and pour in the beans. Boil for 3–4 minutes, then drain, and soak in cold water for 2 hours. Drain again, and put in a saucepan, cover with water, and add the thyme, the bay leaf, one of the garlic cloves, sliced, the onion and seasoning. Cover and bring to the boil, then simmer for 1–2 hours, until tender. Add more water if necessary, but by the time they are cooked, the water should have become a small amount of creamy liquid, in which the beans are served. Stir in hazelnut oil to taste, add the chopped parsley and remaining clove of chopped garlic, and serve. These beans are often served as an accompaniment to roast lamb.

GRAINES DE CAPUCINES AU VINAIGRE

Pickled Nasturtium Seeds

Both the peppery leaves and the flowers of nasturtiums can be used in salads, and when the flowers have died, the seeds can be picked and used like capers. Gather them soon after the seedheads have formed. (Illustrated above)

enough nasturtium seeds to fill a jam jar
coarse salt
about 20 whole peppercorns
sprig of tarragon
2 or 3 shallots
1 garlic clove, peeled
white wine vinegar

Put the seeds on a plate, and cover with salt. Leave until the following day, then drain and rinse them. Place the rinsed seeds in a glass jar, adding the peppercorns, tarragon, shallots and garlic as you fill the jar, so that they are evenly distributed. Fill up the jar with wine vinegar, cover tightly, and place on a sunny window-ledge for 3 weeks.

SALADE AUX GIROLLES TIEDES

Salad of Warm Girolle Mushrooms

After summer or autumn rain, the woods of Périgord are alive with mushroom hunters. After the cep, the apricot-yellow girolle or chanterelle is the most sought-after woodland mushroom, easily recognized not only by its bright colour, but also by its trumpet-shaped cap, yellow gills and tapering stem. Unlike the cep, it is easy to distinguish from poisonous varieties, but if you are in France it is always advisable to check with a local pharmacist, who will usually be very happy to give an expert opinion.

Girolles, with their delicate, slightly peppery flavour and firm texture, are quite the most delicious of mushrooms. Here, they are sautéed with garlic and parsley, and served warm. Avocados, though not native to Périgord or a part of its traditional cuisine, are now seen on market stalls everywhere.

SERVES 4
675g/1½lb fresh girolles
1 avocado (optional)
2 garlic cloves, chopped
1tbsp chopped parsley
1 tomato, peeled, deseeded and diced
100g/3½oz cooked ham, diced
mixed salad leaves
2tbsp walnut oil
2tbsp broken toasted walnuts or pine nuts
salt and freshly ground black pepper

Clean the girolles, preferably without washing them, as they tend to absorb water. Remove any bits of debris or soil with a small, soft brush, such as a pastry brush. Cut any large mushrooms in half lengthwise, but leave the rest whole.

Peel the avocado, if using, cut the flesh into cubes and brush with lemon juice to prevent it from going brown.

Heat the oil in a large pan, and throw the girolles into the hot oil. Stir over high heat for a few minutes, taking care that they do not burn, then season with salt and pepper, turn down the heat and add the garlic, parsley, tomato and ham. Cover the pan, and leave over a gentle heat for 10 minutes while you prepare the salad.

Dress the salad leaves lightly with walnut oil, and arrange either in a serving dish or on individual plates. Scatter with the avocado cubes if using, and the toasted walnuts or pine nuts. When the girolles are ready, spoon on top of the salad and serve while still warm.

SOBRONNADE

Stew of White Beans, Pork and Vegetables

Sometimes described as a soup, this hearty blend of haricot beans and pork is more of a thick stew, in which you should be able to stand a wooden spoon, according to La Mazille in her book La Bonne Cuisine du Périgord, *published in 1929. Like many of the dishes of Périgord, this recipe evolved from the need to put food to cook before going out to work in the fields, and to return to a meal that would satisfy keen appetites; it could be set over a fire and left to bubble away until lunchtime.*

SERVES 6–8
450g/1lb belly of pork, diced
1tbsp goose fat
3 large carrots, peeled and sliced
1 large or 2 small onions, peeled and stuck with 2 cloves

2 turnips, peeled and thinly sliced
450g/1lb dried haricot beans, soaked overnight in water
bouquet garni
1 large potato, peeled and sliced
115g/4oz smoked ham, diced
persillade made from 3 garlic cloves, finely chopped, and one bunch of fresh parsley, chopped
salt and freshly ground black pepper

Fry the diced pork until brown in goose fat. Add carrots, onion, and turnips, cook for another 20 minutes, then add the drained, soaked beans, and cover with 1.5l/2½pt fresh water. Season with salt and pepper, add the bouquet garni, and bring to the boil. Remove any scum that rises to the surface.

Simmer gently, covered, for about 1½ hours, then add the sliced potato and the ham. After another hour, both potato and beans should be beginning to break apart, thickening the broth. Stir in the *persillade*, adjust seasoning, cook for another 10 minutes, then serve, poured over thick slices of crusty bread.

POULE AU POT, SAUCE SORGES

Poached Chicken with Egg and Herb Sauce

This great classic of French cookery is served at La Chouette Gourmande, near Nontron, with a sauce attributed by La Mazille to the tiny village of Sorges, in the Périgord Blanc. Although Sorges is best known for its truffle museum and plantations of truffières, *la sauce de Sorges contains no truffles; in fact, it is a mustardy vinaigrette thickened with the yolks of hard-boiled eggs, and flavoured with herbs.*

SERVES 6
1 free-range chicken, weighing about 2kg/4½lb
a mixture of vegetables such as carrots, leeks, turnips and celery
1 onion, stuck with a clove
bouquet garni
2–3 sprigs of young nettles, chopped (optional)

FOR THE SAUCE
2 eggs
1tsp mustard
1tbsp vinegar
3tbsp sunflower or grapeseed oil
1 shallot, very finely chopped
a handful of freshly chopped herbs such as parsley, tarragon, chervil and chives
salt and freshly ground black pepper

Place the chicken in a large pot of seasoned water, cover, and bring to the boil. Simmer gently for an hour, then add the vegetables and the onion, peeled and trimmed but left whole. Cover again, and cook for at least another hour. Towards the end of the cooking time, add the chopped nettles, if using.

While the chicken is cooking, hard-boil the 2 eggs, then peel them. Cut the eggs in half, scoop out the yolks, and mash these with a fork. Chop the whites and set aside. Mix the mustard, vinegar and mashed yolks together, then add the oil, bit by bit, whisking constantly so that the mixture emulsifies, and season to taste. Add the chopped shallot, chopped herbs and egg whites, and mix well.

To serve, lift out the chicken and vegetables from the liquid (keep this for soup), cut into portions, and serve with the sauce.

DAUBE DE SANGLIER AUX CHATAIGNES

Casserole of Wild Boar with Chestnuts

At the end of the season, hunters gather for a celebratory feast, and wild boar, le sanglier, is usually the highlight of the menu. The young marcassins, as they are called, are tender enough to be roasted, but older beasts are cooked en daube, *with wine and onions. Wild boar meat can be difficult to find, but free-range pork can be used instead.*

SERVES 6
2 tbsp goose fat
3 large onions, finely chopped
3 garlic cloves, chopped
900g/2lb boar meat, from the leg, cut into
5cm/2in cubes
55g/2oz flour
1 bottle white wine
bouquet garni
450g/1lb fresh chestnuts
salt and freshly ground black pepper

Preheat the oven to 160°C/325°F/gas mark 3. Heat half of the goose fat in a large frying pan, and cook the onions until golden. Add the garlic, stir and cook briefly. Remove the onions and garlic and set aside. Coat the pieces of meat in seasoned flour, shake off any excess, add the remaining fat to the frying pan, and when hot, brown the meat on all sides.

Transfer half the onions to a casserole, place the meat on top, then cover with more onions. Pour the wine into the frying pan, and bring to the boil, scraping all of the meaty bits into the liquid. Pour over the meat, add the bouquet garni, season, and cover tightly. Transfer to the oven and cook for at least 3 hours.

While the meat is cooking, prepare the chestnuts. Score the skin of each down one side with a sharp knife, and cover with cold water. Bring to the boil, simmer for 2 minutes, then drain and peel while still hot. If the inner skin does not come away, put the chestnuts back into the saucepan, cover with water, and bring once more to the boil. This should loosen the skins enough to peel them easily. About 45 minutes before the end of the meat's cooking time, add the chestnuts to the casserole.

CIVET DE CHEVREUIL

Casserole of Venison in Red Wine

The forests of Périgord were once filled with wild game, which frequently appeared on the menu at grand banquets. Today, the venison and wild boar that feature on restaurant menus are more likely to have been raised in semi-captivity, probably fenced inside a reserve but with plenty of space to roam around.

Combined with the flavours of wild thyme and juniper, both of which are found in great abundance on the limestone causses, *and cooked slowly until it is tender, venison makes a wonderful dish for winter. In this dish, it is marinated in red wine before cooking, and served with pickled cherries sweetened with a little redcurrant jelly.*

SERVES 4–5

FOR THE MARINADE
400ml/14fl oz robust red wine, such as
Pécharmant
3tbsp olive oil
4 juniper berries, crushed
2 garlic cloves, sliced
a sprig of thyme

bay leaf
salt and freshly ground pepper

FOR THE CASSEROLE
1kg/2¼lb shoulder or haunch of venison,
cut in chunks
2tbsp goose fat
115g/4oz streaky bacon, diced
12 small onions
250g/8½oz small chestnut mushrooms
1tbsp seasoned flour
2 carrots, diced
12 pickled cherries and their juice (optional)
2tbsp redcurrant jelly (optional)
2 cloves garlic

Start the day before you wish to serve the casserole. Put all the marinade ingredients, together with the venison, into a bowl, mix well, and leave in a cool place for at least 6 hours, preferably 24.

When you are ready to start cooking, strain the marinade off the meat. Heat the goose fat in a flameproof casserole and brown the bacon until the fat starts to run. With a slotted spoon, remove it to a plate, then brown the onions with the garlic, and then the mushrooms in turn, and lift them out on to another plate. Put seasoned flour into a plastic bag, and place the drained meat in the bag, shaking until coated with flour. Shake off excess flour. Next brown the venison in the fat, and then add the marinade liquid, carrots, bacon, onions and mushrooms. If there is not enough liquid to cover the meat, add beef stock or water. Cover tightly, and cook slowly, either on the hob, or in a low oven, 150°C/300°F/gas mark 2, for 3½–4 hours. At the end of the cooking time, if there is too much liquid, strain it into another pan and reduce. Stir in a dozen pickled cherries and 2 tablespoons of redcurrant jelly, pour back over the meat, and serve.

COMPOTE DE PIGEONS AUX PETITS POIS

Casserole of Pigeon with Young Peas

Country people of Périgord and Quercy have many cunning ways of trapping wild pigeons, while the ubiquitous pigeonniers to be seen around the region are a testament to the once widespread practice of rearing pigeons for the table. Today, however, pigeonniers are more likely to be used as rooms for renting out to visitors than for raising pigeons. But specialist producers rear pigeonneaux – young birds fed on maize and other types of grain – which, because they are prevented from flying, are exceptionally plump and tender. Known as squabs, these farm-raised pigeons are almost twice the size of wild ones. (illustrated right)

SERVES 4
1tbsp goose fat or oil
85g/3oz salt belly pork, diced
4 pigeons or squabs
12 tiny onions
1 dessertspoon plain flour
150ml/5fl oz white wine, mixed with an equal quantity of water
bouquet garlic of bay leaf, thyme and parsley, tied together
285g/10oz petits pois, shelled weight

In a cast-iron casserole or saucepan with a lid, heat the fat or oil, and brown the salt pork for 5 minutes. Add the pigeons, and cook for 10 minutes or so, turning several times. When browned all over, remove the pork and birds with a slotted spoon, and set aside. Put the whole peeled onions into the pan, and cook for a few minutes, until starting to brown, then remove them to the same dish as the pigeons.

Using the fat in which you have cooked the pork, pigeons and onions, make a roux with the flour, and gradually stir in the wine and water. Bring back to the boil, stirring constantly to prevent lumps forming. Add the bouquet garni, replace the other ingredients, and cover the pot with a lid.

Simmer very gently over low heat for about 1 hour, or until the meat is tender, then add the peas to the pot. Cook for around another 10 minutes, taste the sauce and adjust the seasoning if necessary, then serve. If the sauce tastes too acidic, stir in a teaspoon of sugar just before serving.

MOUSSE AUX CHATAIGNES ET AU CHOCOLAT

Chestnut and Chocolate Mousse

Chestnuts and chocolate are a favourite combination in périgourdin cooking, and this mousse is a variation on the theme. The quality of the chocolate is important: it should be as dark and bitter as possible. Use canned chestnut purée if you are in a hurry.

SERVES 6
150g/5½oz dark bitter chocolate
450g/1lb unsweetened chestnut purée
3tbsp caster sugar
3 eggs, separated
2 heaped tbsp crème fraîche or whipped cream
dash of chestnut liqueur or brandy

Melt the chocolate in a bowl set over a pan of simmering water, keeping back 2 squares. Beat the chestnut purée with 2 tablespoons of sugar (this can be done in an electric blender).

Whisk the egg yolks with the remaining sugar until pale and creamy, then stir into the hot chocolate, off the heat, mixing quickly until they are completely blended and partially cooked. Leave to cool, then stir in the chestnut purée, crème fraîche and liqueur.

Whisk the egg whites until stiff, then fold into the chestnut and chocolate mixture, using a metal spoon or whisk. Work as lightly as possible, so that the foam does not collapse. As soon as the egg whites are absorbed, pour the mousse into individual ramekins, or a decorative serving dish, then refrigerate for at least 4 hours. Decorate with a little whipped cream and grated chocolate.

TARTE AUX FRAISES

Strawberry Tart

Made with pâté sucrée, crème pâtissière and the freshest strawberries, this is one of the finest fruit tarts. (Illustrated right)

SERVES 6
400g/14oz strawberrries
100g/3½oz cold, unsalted butter, cut into small cubes
200g/7oz plain flour
100g/3½oz icing sugar
6 egg yolks

FOR THE CREME PATISSIERE
350ml/12fl oz milk
4 egg yolks
75g/2½oz caster sugar
30g/1oz flour
a few drops of vanilla essence
4tbsp redcurrant jelly, to glaze

To make the pastry, rub the butter into the flour with your fingertips, until the texture is like coarse crumbs. Add the other ingredients, and work together into a smooth dough. Press this dough into a ball, wrap in film and chill for 30 minutes.

Preheat the oven to 220°C/425°F/gas mark 7. To make the *crème pâtissière*, bring the milk to the boil. Whisk the egg yolks with sugar until light and creamy, then whisk in the flour. Strain the milk on to the egg yolks and sugar, and whisk vigorously to prevent lumps forming. Pour back into the saucepan, and bring to the boil, stirring. Simmer gently for about 3 minutes, still stirring, then add the vanilla essence. Strain into a bowl, cover and chill.

Roll out the pastry, and use to line a greased 25cm/10in tart tin with a removable base. Chill

again for 20 minutes before baking blind for 10 minutes, then reduce the heat to 190°C/375°F/gas mark 5, and bake for a further 15 minutes. Cool slightly in the tin before unmoulding.

Pour the cool *crème pâtissière* into the pastry shell, then arrange the halved strawberries on top. Dissolve the redcurrant jelly with a tablespoon of water over gentle heat, and brush it over the fruit to glaze it.

Serve warm or cold, within 2 hours.

GATEAU DE MIEL ET NOISETTES

Honey and Hazelnut Cake

'After half an hour in the oven, you will smell the heady fragrance of this rustic cake,' says La Mazille, 'an aroma in which Virgil himself would have taken delight.'

SERVES 6–8
225g/8oz runny honey
5 eggs, separated
½tsp vanilla essence
2tbsp hazelnut oil or single cream
100g/3½oz hazelnuts, toasted, with skins rubbed off
100g/3½oz plain flour

Preheat the oven to 180°C/350°F/gas mark 4. Soften the honey by heating gently. Beat the egg yolks, and whisk in the runny honey until the mixture becomes light and creamy. Add the vanilla essence and the oil or cream. Grind the hazelnuts, taking care not to over-process. Sift the flour into the egg mixture, and gradually incorporate the ground hazelnuts. Whisk the egg whites until stiff, and fold in carefully. Pour the mixture into a greased 20cm/8in cake tin and bake for 30–40 minutes.

SORBET AUX FLEURS DE SUREAU

Elderflower Sorbet

La Bonne Cuisine du Périgord, *written by La Mazille, played a leading part in Micheline Dupin's decision to leave Paris and open a small country restaurant in the Dordogne, where she would serve dishes described in the book. She called it La Chouette Gourmande, because she noticed that the woods around her house were full of owls. One of the pleasures of eating and staying at La Chouette Gourmande is the feeling that you have been invited into a private home: all of the food is home-made and the set menu (right) changes daily.*

Micheline Dupin likes to serve light, fresh desserts at La Chouette Gourmande, to offset the richness of a traditional périgourdin dinner. Fruit from the garden is accompanied by a seasonal sorbet: in June there are plentiful elderflowers, and later, rose petals. Both have a wonderfully refreshing fragrance. (Sorbets illustrated left)

She serves sorbet with croquants d'anis, *little biscuits flavoured with aniseed.*

SERVES 4–6
25g/³⁄₄oz elderflowers
125g/4¹⁄₂oz sugar
zest and juice of 2 lemons
1 egg white

Pick the elderflowers (preferably from a traffic-free zone) when they are fully open and at their peak of fragrance. Cut off the stems and weigh the flowers.

Dissolve the sugar in 500ml/16fl oz water, add elderflowers, lemon zest and juice, and bring slowly to the boil. Simmer for 1 minute, then take off the heat and leave to infuse for 15 minutes. Strain and put the syrup into the deep freeze, in a plastic or metal container, for several hours.

When half-frozen, and full of ice crystals, remove from the freezer, and beat, together with the egg white, in a food processor or with a hand whisk, until the mixture is the consistency of stiff egg whites. Pour back into the container, and freeze again for at least an hour, until required. The sorbet will retain its fragrance for several days in the freezer, but not much longer.

Rose-petal sorbet can be made in exactly the same way, using 55g/2oz of red rose petals, of a highly perfumed variety, and picked before the petals begin to fall. Serve the sorbet with raspberries, strawberries, red- or whitecurrants, or poached gooseberries, and *croquants*.

CROQUANTS

Aniseed Biscuits

2 eggs
100g/3½oz sugar
100g/3½oz flour
2tbsp double cream
sprig of anise leaves, chopped, *or* **1tsp**
aniseeds
butter, for greasing

Preheat the oven to 200°C/400°F/gas mark 6. Whisk the eggs with the sugar, then blend in the flour and cream. Beat vigorously until the mixture is completely smooth, then add the anise leaves or seeds.

Butter a baking sheet, and place a teaspoon of mixture on the tray. Bake the biscuits for 10–15 minutes, until golden brown. Allow to cool before serving. (Illustrated right)

FLAUGNARDE AUX POIRES

Périgourdin *Pear Flan*

This light périgourdin *version of its more famous* Limousin cousin, le clafoutis, *(which uses* griotte cherries), *is more usually made with prunes, plums or grapes; this recipe uses pears, which have a particular lightness and delicacy. It is at its best if served warm, or at least at room temperature.*

SERVES 4
3 eggs
100g/3½oz plain flour
300ml/10fl oz full-cream milk
1tbsp rum or pear liqueur
1tsp orange flower water
3tbsp vanilla sugar
2 ripe pears
45g/1½oz unsalted butter
icing sugar, to finish

Preheat the oven to 200°C/400°F/gas mark 6. Put the eggs into a large bowl and beat together. Sift the flour with a pinch of salt over the beaten eggs. Whisk the mixture well, then add the milk, rum, orange flower water and sugar. Alternatively, blend in a food processor or electric blender, adding the sugar at the end, after the other ingredients have been combined.

Peel the pears, and cut into dice. Butter a 23cm/9in cake tin generously, then arrange the pear pieces evenly over the bottom of the tin. Give the batter mixture a final whisk, pour it into the tin over the pears, and dot the surface with the remaining butter. Place the cake tin in the hot oven immediately, and bake for 40–45 minutes, until well risen and golden brown. Remove from the oven, dust with icing sugar, and serve warm.

ABOVE *The red-tiled roofs of Cahors, capital of Quercy, overlooked by the cathedral of Saint-Etienne. The city is built on a loop in the River Lot, which is spanned by the Pont Saint-Valentré, a spellbinding feat of medieval engineering. Cahors is best known for its red wine and truffles, but the town has a less famous speciality, les coques de Pâques au cédrat, round brioches containing candied citron peel, traditionally made at Easter.*

RIGHT *Quercy lamb, raised on the limestone causses.*

FAR RIGHT *Dried maize stored in cages called cribs.*

QUERCY

Tucked between Périgord, Gascony and the mountains of Auvergne, three regions well known for their gastronomic riches, the old province of Quercy often gets forgotten on the culinary map of France. It is all a question of identity, and somehow *la cuisine quercynoise* has always been regarded as a paler version of *périgourdin* cooking. Considerably less wealthy than Périgord, and with far fewer chateaux, Quercy never acquired the same reputation for extravagant dishes, even though a great deal of the region's everyday cooking has always had much in common with that of its neighbour. Similarly, its cooking has largely gone unrecorded, while many books and articles have been written on *la bonne cuisine du Périgord* – with the result that almost half of the French population now believe that Périgord, with its Holy Trinity of truffles, ceps and foie gras, is the greatest gastronomic region in France.

This may be so, but you are just as likely to eat well in Quercy. The region has its own gastronomic riches, and in any case, certain *produits du terroir* are disturbingly ubiquitous, and many small farmers in Quercy have turned to fattening ducks and making foie gras and *confit*, like their neighbours in Périgord. Truffles, often associated with the Sarladais in the heart of Périgord Noir, are more likely to come from the oak woodlands around Cahors, and while the most important market for ceps takes place at Villefranche-du-Périgord, most of the mushrooms sold there are gathered in the Bouriane region, in Quercy.

So what is special about the cooking of Quercy? Its strength, like all good cooking, lies in the judicious combination of regional produce, and that includes a whole variety of fruit and vegetables, meat and poultry, not just ducks and truffles. In fact, it is often in the ingenious use of inexpensive and everyday ingredients, rather than the luxuries for which a region becomes famous, that the most appetizing dishes evolve.

Two years ago, the people of Thégra, a pretty village on the Causse de Gramat, produced a collection of traditional local recipes and published them in a booklet on the occasion of the village fête. The recipes have a more than passing resemblance to the classic dishes of Périgord; the significant difference is that no mention is made of foie gras or truffles, except in the stuffing for the Christmas turkey. Instead, it is a litany of ingenuity, revolving around the seasons, and using ingredients that could be produced at home or hunted: rabbit, chicken, pigeon or partridge, stuffed and simply roasted; *boudin* sausage, made with the blood of a freshly killed pig; lamb with haricot beans; stuffed cabbage (see pages 88–9).

TOP The Auxerrois grape gives Cahors wine its robust, rugged quality and a firm backbone of tannin, which enables it to age well. As well as Auxerrois grapes, which make up about 70 per cent of the blend, the wines of Cahors are made from the Tannat grape, which gives structure, and Merlot, with its ripe, red fruit flavours and smooth texture.
ABOVE Top-quality black truffles, at La Maison Pebeyre in Cahors, a bastion of tradition. Four generations of Pebeyres have cultivated, bought and sold truffles throughout the world.

LEFT Sheep grazing in the bottom of a dry valley, in rocky limestone country near Rocamadour.
TOP The famous agneau de Quercy.
ABOVE A picturesque tower in Carennac, an unspoilt village on the banks of the Dordogne, which was once famous for its greengages.

An abhorrence of waste is evident throughout, and there is a strong sense that the best bits of everything would have been sold, leaving, for example, the carcass of a fattened duck to be stuffed with a *mique*, or dumpling, and simmered in bouillon; while the blood would be made into *sanguette* and fried with onions and garlic. Frugality was the order of the day, and dishes like *estouffade* (see page 87) stretched rare treats such as ceps a long way, by padding them out with potatoes. As in Périgord, dumplings, often known here as *fars*, as well as *miques*, were a filling alternative to bread, and a regular feature on the dinner table.

It is not hard to imagine a typical Quercy farm in the early years of this century, with a small flock of sheep and goats, a pig in its sty, the *basse-cour* where poultry scratch and rabbits live in cages, and a well-tended kitchen garden with a few fruit trees. Virtually all of the traditional dishes of the region could be made with the produce from such a farm, supplemented with the results of the odd hunting and gathering expedition. Delicious soups, or *tourains*, made from garlic or onions with added tomatoes (see page 86), sorrel or turnips, and thickened with egg; freshly gathered salad leaves livened up with a few pieces of ham (see page 60); rabbit casserole with prunes (see page 90); or the celebrated *pastis quercynoise* (see page 93), a feather-light confection of thin layers of pastry with an apple filling – none of these require fancy ingredients, and all are unusually good.

Today, these small mixed farms have a struggle to survive, but many farmers have found that they can make ends meet by running restaurants and *ferme-auberges* serving traditional food alongside the farm.

FOOD FROM THE CAUSSES

Much of Quercy consists of upland limestone areas, known as the *causses*, which have an austere and wild beauty. Signs of the rural exodus are evident in the landscape: drystone walls are often in a tumbledown state, while mellow old farmhouses, with pigeonniers and exterior stone staircases, frequently have an abandoned air about them. Only some have been restored with such dedication and respect for tradition as the farm buildings at La Petite Auberge at Lascabanes (see page 83).

This limestone scenery includes some spectacular caves and canyons. The village of Rocamadour, which had its heyday as a centre of pilgrimage in the thirteenth century, clings to the precipitous rock face of one such canyon. It now attracts even greater numbers of visitors, not all of them pilgrims. Sheep and goats thrive on the aromatic herbs and grasses that grow on this arid land, and Rocamadour has given its name to the little goats' cheese that is made in the region, *cabécou de Rocamadour*, recently granted an *appellation contrôlée*.

Cabécou, which means 'little goats' cheese' in the patois *langue d'oc*, is in fact made all over Périgord and Quercy, but only that from a specially delineated region around Rocamadour is entitled to the appellation. Although varying slightly from place to place, the cheeses are always tiny, rarely weighing more than 45g/1½oz, and are sold at different stages of maturity, from *frais*, only 48 hours old, to sec, at 15 days, when they are quite strong and pungent. Between the two there are *crémeux* and *moelleux*. Sometimes the cheeses are macerated in

CHARCUTERIE

Quercy is not a region best known for its charcuterie, but in the past most families raised a pig, and made their own hams, bacon and sausages. Today, most people buy charcuterie from a specialist shop or supermarket, but a few still make their own.
Patrick and Pascale Duler of La Petite Auberge at Lascabanes (see page 83) are amongst them, and some of their produce is shown above.
For preserved pork, they raise black Gascon pigs, and make (clockwise from bottom right) le jambon cru au sel sec *(air-dried ham) which takes many months to mature, and is eaten raw;* la poitrine roulée, *a kind of bacon which is added to stews of leaner meat to provide a contrast of flavour and texture;* la rosette, *a salami-type sausage which is eaten raw;* la saucisse sèche, *which is sliced and served as an hors d'oeuvre with pickled gherkins* (cornichons); *and* le saucisson, *which is smaller than* la rosette, *but otherwise the same. Duck breast, or* magret de canard, *is salted and dried like ham, then smoked.* Magret fumé *is served thinly sliced, in the same way as ham.*

CABECOU

Two kilometres north of Rocamadour, in wild, rocky country, is the hamlet of Les Alix, where the Lacoste family have been making cabécou goats' cheese since 1920. In the tiny dairy beneath her 12th-century stone farmhouse, Marcelle Lacoste makes about 500 little chèvres every day, while her son Alain takes care of the herd of 100 Alpine goats.

The warm milk has rennet added, and when the curds have set, it is drained for a day. Mme Lacoste then kneads the curd, presses it into moulds, and sets the tiny discs to mature on racks, where they are turned daily. Each litre of milk produces only three cabécous.

The cheeses can be eaten fresh within 48 hours of making, but they are usually sold after about eight days, when they are described as crémeux. At 15 days, they are très sec, and very strong in flavour. Twice a week, the Lacostes send a consignment of cabécous to a select list of restaurants in Paris.

plum eau-de-vie, and called *cabécou truffé*. In the past, they were eaten just as they are, with bread, but in recent years, people have taken to serving them grilled on toast, with salad leaves, either as a starter or as the cheese course.

Once known for its sheep fairs, the town of Gramat has given its name to a hardy, prolific breed of sheep with white fleece and black rings around the eyes, which look as if they are wearing sunglasses. Another local species is the Causses du Lot, which is also especially well adapted to the difficult conditions on the causses. Fed on mother's milk, summer grass and hay in winter, *agneau de Quercy* is marketed under the Label Rouge name, which guarantees certain standards of rearing, slaughtering and butchering. Each piece of meat has an 'identity card', from which it is possible to trace its origin.

There are many local ways of cooking the tender meat: studded with garlic and roasted with thyme and juniper; in rich, slow-cooked daubes, with onions, tomatoes and red Cahors wine; or cooked on a spit in front of the fire, and served with an *estouffat* of white haricot beans.

The Causse de Martel centres on the medieval town of Martel, known as the 'town of seven towers', where each Saturday a lively market is held in the Place des Consuls beneath the eighteenth-century *halles*. This is a real neighbourhood market, friendly and convivial, where *petits producteurs* sell the produce from their own farm or smallholding: walnuts, asparagus, Jerusalem artichokes or other seasonal vegetables; honey, flowers and farm-raised chickens, as well as fresh farmhouse cheeses, made just a few miles away.

Market day is rounded off by a short trip out of town, for on Saturday afternoons the walnut mill at Les Landes is open. Cloth-capped farmers bring along their walnuts in sacks and plastic bags to be put through the mill while they wait, then collect their newly-pressed oil a few hours later in old wine or water bottles. For those without their own walnut trees, the golden, fragrant oil is also sold ready-bottled.

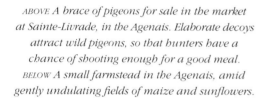

ABOVE La Charcuterie Ponthoreau, in the town of Tonneins, on the banks of the Garonne, is the source of a local speciality, le véritable jambon de Tonneins, *a succulent mixture of chunks of leg and shoulder of pork, flavoured with garlic and spices, and cooked very slowly so that it becomes enveloped in a delicious jelly. It can be eaten hot or cold, and can even be bought by mail order. Reputed to have been a favourite of Louis XIII, its history goes back a long way. Other Ponthoreau specialities include* boudin, confit de dinde *and* jambonneau farci.
LEFT A black Gascon pig enjoying the sunshine.
BELOW Beehives are a common sight in Quercy, often placed amongst the plum trees so that both honey and prunes can be produced from the same orchard. This one is in woodland on the causses.

ABOVE A brace of pigeons for sale in the market at Sainte-Livrade, in the Agenais. Elaborate decoys attract wild pigeons, so that hunters have a chance of shooting enough for a good meal.
BELOW A small farmstead in the Agenais, amid gently undulating fields of maize and sunflowers.

ON THE SCENT OF THE BLACK TRUFFLE

Surrounded by mystery, the black truffle, *Tuber melanosporum*, has always been a source of intense fascination for anyone remotely interested in gastronomy. Its first curiosity is its blackness, hardly appetizing in the normal run of things, then there is the way it grows – in the poorest of soils, and underground, out of sight. Perhaps its most intriguing aspect is its price – what is it that persuades people to part with such exorbitant sums for the sake of a small, unprepossessing fungus with a very strong smell?

Sadly, for many of us, the first encounter with a truffle is disappointing, because we expect the world of that tiny black stud in the middle of a piece of foie gras or pâté, and it turns out to be nothing at all. The trouble is that you can't economize with truffles, and a commercially made pâté that has been prepared with profit in mind, rather than enjoyment, is probably not worth the money. Impecunious truffle-seekers are better advised to borrow a truffle if they can, and put it in a jar with half a dozen eggs for a day, then to scramble the eggs and return the truffle to its owner. That way you can appreciate its extraordinary aroma, which is what all the fuss is about, for free. Or you could go to the truffle market at Lalbenque and just smell the air.

Black truffles grow in the scrubby oak woodland around the town of Lalbenque, in the Causse de Limogne, and it is here that Quercy's most famous truffle market takes place. On normal days very little happens in Lalbenque, but on Tuesdays between the end of November and the beginning of March, a change takes place and the main street suddenly fills with crowds of excited people. Most of them pile into the Hôtel Lion d'Or to lunch on a typical meal of home-made *pâté de campagne*, *céleri remoulade* and tomato salad, *rôti de porc* and *haricots blancs*, followed by cheese and *pastis quercynois* (see page 93). The room buzzes with the sound of animated conversation.

As lunch draws to an end, country people line up behind trestle tables in the main street, each with a small basket in front of them containing the truffles, wrapped in a cloth. At the sound of a bell, at 2.30pm precisely, well-dressed buyers appear and the air is filled with the whisper of prices – 3000F, 4000F, 5000F a kilogram. Much of the bargaining is done on trust, because buyers are not permitted to touch the truffles, and an unscrupulous seller could easily conceal lumps of earth below the top layer in the basket. As it is the custom for the buyer to take the entire contents of the basket, a small lump of mud could make a difference of several hundred francs. But deals are struck, and when the truffles are sold, the cloth is folded over again to avoid any confusion. Outside the Mairie, on the opposite side of the road, a magnificent set of weighing scales is occasionally used to settle any disputes.

Buying truffles is a risky business, even for the experts. A good black truffle should be firm to the touch: if too soft, it may have been frozen and have rotted; if too hard, it may be woody. It should not be too light in weight, which would indicate that it is dehydrated, nor should it smell sour, which means that it has been soaked in water to restore it. It should have a powerful aroma; if it does not, it may be an immature summer truffle. The best advice for amateur enthusiasts is to buy bottled truffles from a reputable supplier, such as Pebeyre in Cahors, or to be content to eat truffles in restaurants.

A young sow, la truie, which has been specially trained to detect the scent of black truffles even when they are well below the surface of the soil. The pig is fed tiny morsels of truffle until she recognizes its pungent scent, then taught to search for hidden pieces of tuber melanosporum, and rewarded with food when she makes a successful find.

THE TRUFFLE MARKET

*Although black truffles are sold in markets
throughout Quercy and Périgord, those in the
trade go to buy in the village of Lalbenque in the
Causse de Limogne, one of the half-dozen
surviving professional truffle markets in France.
Every Tuesday afternoon during the season,
a large crowd of buyers and interested observers
gathers outside the Town Hall as vendors
display their baskets, brimming over with truffles.*

*Prices are governed entirely by the law of supply
and demand, and although it looks chaotic,
the market is in fact highly organized. Each
dealer or* courtier *has a special relationship with
several producers, and fraud is rare.
M. Cavaleur, a member of the Confrérie du
Diamant Noir, which represents producers,
tests out a truffle (right, above).*

ASPARAGUS

For the Delpech family, Saturday and Sunday are not days of rest. They grow asparagus, and on Saturday afternoons can be found in the packing-shed behind their cottage, engaged in the time-consuming process of washing, trimming, grading and tying the purple-white shoots into neat bundles, ready for the busy Sunday morning market at Agen. Many producers now send their crop to the factory, which cuts down the amount of labour, but the Delpech family prefer to do things in the traditional way, and to maintain direct contact with their customers. From time to time, friends and neighbours turn up to buy asparagus for Sunday lunch, and to catch up on the gossip while they make their purchase.

The season lasts from mid-April until the feast of Saint Jean (24th June). Every day young Gérard Delpech scours the furrows for signs of a purple-blue spear about to break the surface of the soil. To the unaccustomed eye, this achievement seems like a minor miracle, as often the only clue is a slight cracking of the earth. Using his sharpened gouge, a tool specially designed to cut the stems cleanly right down at their underground base, he deftly cuts and lifts the tender shoot and places it in the basket. They will be covered with soil, especially after rain, and although this makes work later, it also means that the spears will keep in perfect condition for several days if refrigerated.

On the eve of the twice-weekly market, the preparation process starts in earnest. First, the spears are soaked for an hour or so in water to loosen the dirt, then they are scraped to remove the tough outer skin. Next, they are graded and trimmed, then washed again and tied into bunches. The bigger spears fetch higher prices, while the slender points of broken stems are sold to restaurants.

A WOODLAND HARVEST

High up to the east of Saint-Céré, on the flanks of the Massif Central, is the area known as La Châtaignerie, named for its chestnut forests. With acid soil and a cool, damp climate, more demanding crops, such as wheat and maize, are reluctant to grow, and chestnuts were initially planted to provide food not only for animals, but also for the peasants. Before potatoes arrived from the New World, a meal consisting of nothing but boiled chestnuts was a regular occurrence for these poor farmers – a far cry from the costly boxes of *marrons glacés* that people now enjoy as a luxurious confection. Chestnuts were also made into flour for bread and cakes, and used in soups, stews and stuffings, as they still are today.

To the north of the Lot valley, and to the west of the RN20, is a region that belongs more in character to the Périgord than to Quercy, known as the Bouriane. Almost entirely covered by tall pine, oak and chestnut trees, the Bouriane has a damp climate that encourages the growth not only of trees, but also of fungi, and people travel from far away to search for ceps and chanterelles in the season.

Although the mushroom season is usually early autumn, summer rainfall can stimulate early growth and cause them to spring up everywhere during June, July or August. Suddenly the woods become alive with people shuffling furtively through the undergrowth with baskets over their arms in search of mushrooms. As well as making an appearance at local markets, such as Prayssac, vast quantities of ceps and chanterelles from the Bouriane are sent to Paris, and exported to Brussels and the mushroom-hungry cities of Germany.

FRESH FROM THE MARKET

The Friday market at Prayssac is one of the most colourful of the many markets taking place in Quercy. In summertime, about 60 *petits producteurs* sell their home-grown produce beneath the shady chestnut trees that grow around the church. Produce comes from near and far: strings of fresh purple garlic from Lomagne, 100 kilometres away in the Gers, sold by Jeannot Marcel, whose handwritten notice proudly proclaims that '*l'ail est comme le vin; il a ses terrains; nos terres sont pour cette culture*' (garlic is like wine; it grows well on certain soils, and ours are the best); punnets of jewel-like red- and blackcurrants, tiny *fraises-des-bois* and juicy Gariguette strawberries from Boudy-de-Beauregard, in the Agenais. From Lauzerte come scented *melons de coteaux*, and from close to Villeneuve-sur-Lot, a mature cows' milk cheese called Palanchou.

Most of the produce comes from closer to home, however, from the rich farmland bordering the River Lot. Courgette flowers, each still clinging to its own baby courgette, patty-pan squashes, tiny *cornichons* for pickling, *coco rouges* – haricot beans with pink mottled skins, sweet *reine-claude* greengages – everywhere you look, some delight catches your eye.

ABOVE RIGHT The market at Villeneuve-sur-Lot: fresh produce in picturesque surroundings.
RIGHT Marmande is famous for its sweet tomatoes, seen here in serried ranks of vivid red.

PIGEONNIERS

*Domestic pigeons, being prolific breeders, provide
a useful source of food; a single pair of pigeons
can produce eight pairs of birds in a year. In the
past, the birds were valued for their droppings,
which were used as fertilizer both for crops and
vegetable gardens, in an area with relatively
few cattle to supply manure.*

To house the birds, pigeonniers *were built in
a bewildering variety of shapes and styles: some
circular, like the double-roofed one at
Coulaures, near Excideuil (far right); some
hexagonal such as the timber-framed example
at Queyssac (right); some square, as in the Quercy,
near Lalbenque (below), and others forming an
integral part of the farmhouse, like the one
at Pont Carral (below right) near Gourdon. In
most regions of France, the ownership of
a* pigeonnier *was a nobleman's privilege, but in
Quercy and Périgord, this right was granted
to anyone who had enough land to support the
birds. The farmers obviously loved their
dovecots and took great pride in their building,
decorating them with delicate cupolas,
ornate finials and finely carved stonework.*

Several stalls sell only organically grown fruit and vegetables; Steef Hogeland, a naturalized Dutchman, has brought his native expertise to grow white aubergines, spaghetti squash, yellow courgettes and tiny, yellow 'light-bulb' tomatoes. From just over the river, at Blaye, come soft goats' cheeses, both rounds and pyramids, as well as *fromage blanc* and *tomme de vache* (pressed cows' milk cheese). Small wonder that Alexis Pélissou, chef-patron of one of Quercy's best restaurants, Le Gindreau (see pages 84–5), insists on shopping here.

Another thriving produce market that is well worth a visit is the one at Villeneuve-sur-Lot; it takes place in the central square every Saturday. Across the river, on Wednesday mornings, there is a more unusual market, the *marché biologique*, where all of the fruit and vegetables, dairy produce and bread, cakes and preserves, have been produced under the umbrella of *Nature et Progrès*, or one of the other organic labels in France. Something of a flagship, the Villeneuve organic market was the first to open on a regular basis outside Paris.

Twenty years ago, Jan Demaître set up a stall at Villeneuve, selling his organic sourdough bread baked in a wood-fired oven. Made with wholewheat flour, spring water and unrefined sea salt, and risen very gently over many hours, 'le Pain Maître' is made without the addition of yeast, and has a wonderfully nutty, full flavour and firm texture. A one-time Belgian academic, who came south with his family to escape the rat-race, Jan Demaître is a typical representative of the organic movement. He bought a ruined chateau, and started to bake bread in the 200-year-old bread oven. Within a short time, his bread had become so popular that he found himself driving thousands of kilometres every week to deliver it. So he moved to Bordeaux, where he now has a shop and supplies the smartest restaurants, as well as sending deliveries to the Wednesday market at Villeneuve.

PRUNE COUNTRY

Although plums are grown throughout Quercy, it is in the Agenais, home of the famous *pruneaux d'Agen*, that the orchards of *prunes d'Ente*, as the purple plums used to make prunes are known, seem to dominate the scene. Indeed, France is the third largest prune-producing country in the world, and almost all come from this area. A vast, monotonous plain, which borders the rivers Lot and Garonne for many miles, the Agenais has fields of maize, sunflowers, tobacco, melons, asparagus and strawberries, as well as plums. To the

PRUNES

In the past, prunes were often dried in the household bread oven, but as demand grew during the early years of the 19th century, specially designed wood-fired étuves, *or drying chambers, came into use. After being sorted and placed on triangular or petal-shaped wickerwork trays called* claies *(above), which were made to fit together like the petals of a flower, the plums were left to dry in the hot sun for a few days. After that, they were subjected to three successive bakings, each one hotter than the last, resulting in a total of 36 hours in the oven. Three kilos of plums are needed to make 1 kilo of prunes.*

Today, the preparation of prunes has been mechanized. Drying ovens operate continuously, and the fruit is loaded on to trolleys, and wheeled into a tunnel, to emerge at the other end when ready. They can then be sealed hermetically in plastic bags and cooked again, so no chemical preservatives are needed.

The whole process can be seen in action at the Prune Museum in Granges-sur-Lot, where there are orchards and a working prune processing plant. A number of old ovens have been reconstructed in the museum, and there is a display of other prune-making paraphernalia, together with a collection of old labels (left) and early packaging. Naturally, the shop sells all manner of prune products, including pruneaux fourrés (far left).

ABOVE AND OPPOSITE Rows of neatly-tended vines at Le Château de Cayrou, owned by the Jouffreau family, who also own Le Clos de Gamot (see far right). Today, it is rare to see grapes being harvested by hand in Cahors, but Jean Jouffreau believes that it is better for the vines to be treated gently. Modern methods are used for vinification, however, which is carried out in stainless steel vats.

north and south of the plain the scenery becomes more interesting, with hillsides dotted with peach and plum trees, which in early spring are a mass of pink and white blossom.

In Britain, prunes are associated with school dinners and considered to be something of a joke, but in France they are regarded with a good deal of relish, and used in all kinds of dishes, both sweet and savoury. Cooked with pork, chicken or rabbit (see page 90), their sweet succulence enriches the sauce and moistens the meat. For dessert, *tarte aux pruneaux* is a regular Sunday treat, usually made with whole, plumped-up prunes, while smaller *tartelettes*, filled with a purée of *crème de pruneaux*, are another favourite (see page 94). Combined with tart apples to balance their natural sweetness, prunes are also made into a deliciously sticky upside-down cake.

Villeneuve-sur-Lot, rather than Agen, has always been the central trading place for prunes, and even today it has several shops entirely devoted to the sale of prunes in all their guises. La Boutique des Pruneaux, close to the Porte de Paris in Villeneuve, displays a spectacular selection of confections on the theme of prunes: *pruneaux fourrés*, stoned and stuffed with rich prune purée, chocolate-coated prunes, chocolates filled with prune liqueur, prunes stuffed with walnuts, prunes in eau-de-vie, and just plain prunes. *Crème de pruneaux* is another speciality, a thick purée which is used in the preparation of patisserie and desserts, and of course there are prune liqueurs and brandies, too.

At Bias, close to Villeneuve-sur-Lot, is Favol's jam factory, where a vast range of preserves are made based originally on local fruit, such as griotte cherries, strawberries, greengages, peaches and apricots. Of course, no fruit processor in this region would be without a selection of prune-based delicacies, and, alongside aperitif snacks such as prunes rolled in bacon or stuffed with cheese, are boxes of *pruneaux fourrés* (shown below), and bottles of prunes in armagnac. More surprisingly, green tomato jam (see page 94) is one of their specialities, and they have recently started to import tropical fruit, so passion fruit, mango and pineapple jams have been added to the list, as well as marmalade. Favol's jams are widely available throughout Quercy and Périgord, but can also be bought direct from the factory.

THE WINES OF CAHORS

Cahors has long been famed for its legendary 'black wines', which travelled well and were particularly appreciated by the English, but when phylloxera struck in 1887, most of the vineyards were abandoned for ever. The winemakers that replanted used hybrid varieties, which resulted in inferior wine, and the region's reputation was lost. In 1956, a very severe frost killed most of these vines, and for several years virtually no wine was produced at all.

Then in the 1960s, a few brave vignerons started to replant with *cépages nobles* – in Cahors, these are the Auxerrois (also known as Cot or Malbec), Merlot and Tannat varieties – and a revival was under way. By 1970, the wines of Cahors had their *appellation contrôlée*, and were once more on the map. Although still rich, robust and dark in colour, they are no longer black, and are made to mature more quickly than they did in the past; which is not necessarily an advantage, but makes better business sense.

CAHORS
APPELLATION CAHORS CONTROLÉE
CLOS DE GAMOT

JOUFFREAU JEAN, PROPRIÉTAIRE-RÉCOLTANT A PRAYSSAC (LOT)
MISE EN BOUTEILLE A LA PROPRIÉTÉ
750 ml ℮   VIN DE FRANCE   12,5 % VOL.
G.M. 10010

LE CLOS DE GAMOT

Jean Jouffreau, owner of Le Clos de Gamot at Prayssac, which has been in his family since 1610, is a great believer in the importance of avoiding chemical fertilizers and weedkillers, preferring to use manure and compost, and to till the vineyards manually to keep down the weeds. He also insists on harvesting the grapes by hand, rather than machine, in order to ensure that only sound, ripe grapes get made into wine.

M. Jouffreau was one of the few to struggle on with wine-making during the 1930s and 40s when the region was in the doldrums and the future looked bleak, and his vines were among the few that survived the terrible frosts of 1956. He is certain that this was due to his old-fashioned methods, which encourage the vines to grow deep roots. He takes pride in making wines that last well, and in the cellars are bottles going back to the last century, which he calls the perpetuelles. *Indeed, his wines are best aged for a few years: they are very tannic when young, but with a little patience they mature to become deep and full-bodied.*

The Auxerrois grape yields tough, austere wine with a strong tannic backbone, softened by the addition of Merlot. The Cahors wines are all red, and when young, should be lightly chilled and eaten with grilled or roasted meat. After three or four years, aromas of pepper and spice develop and the wines become rounded and mellow, making them good company for robust flavours such as game and dishes containing ceps and truffles.

At Château de Haute Serre near the village of Cieurac, south of Cahors, Georges Vigouroux spent three years breaking up boulders on his land with bulldozers before he could plant a single vine. He was convinced that the dry, chalky soil of the *causses* would produce tougher, more long-lasting wines than those grown on the lower slopes that line the Lot valley, and that they would more closely resemble the old Cahors wines. Twenty years on, his wines are indeed in the top league for the region, tough and tannic when young, but with plenty of ripe fruit that lasts well.

The largest producer of Cahors wine, selling 40 per cent of the total amount, is the *cave coopérative*, Les Caves d'Olt, at Parnac. It makes and bottles wine for a variety of properties: Château Legrezette, owned by Alain Perrin, the managing director of Cartier; Château Caix; Château Cayrou d'Albas, Château de Parnac and Château les Bouysses; as well as bottling wine under the name of the co-operative itself. If you are prepared to bottle it yourself, you can also buy quite drinkable everyday wine *en vrac*, pumped out from a large tank, at remarkably low prices.

RIGHT Puy l'Evêque on the River Lot was once a busy river port; narrow streets lined with old houses built of golden stone lead down to the river. The town owes its name to the Bishops of Cahors who once ruled the town.

LE DOMAINE DES SAVARINES

Danielle Biesbrouck, who lives to the south-west of Cahors in a beautiful stone house surrounded by vines, is an enthusiastic convert to biodynamics, an environmentally friendly approach to farming developed by Rudolph Steiner in the 1920s. When she bought Le Domaine des Savarines in 1970, she knew nothing about wine-making, let alone biodynamics, but with the help of Pascal Thiollet, a local oenologist, and a lot of reading, she managed her first bottling in 1978.

She converted to the biodynamic system 12 years later and now uses no chemical weedkillers or pesticides in the vineyards. Instead, she believes in building up a healthy soil structure by using compost, especially that made from nettles, and applying minute quantities of special mineral preparations to the land, rather in the same way as homeopathic medicines are used to treat human disease. All wine-making tasks, including bottling, are done at specified times, on specified dates, according to the phases of the moon and the stars. It all sounds quite bizarre to the uninitiated, but it seems to work, producing smooth yet powerful wines that taste full of fruit. In many ways the system represents a return to traditional methods, and many prominent wine-makers in other parts of France, such as the Leflaive family in Burgundy, are questioning the ever-increasing use of chemicals in wine-making, and experimenting with the biodynamic system.

One of the smallest *vin de pays* appellations in France is the Côteaux de Glanes, which produces just 100,000 bottles of red wine a year. The vines, mainly Merlot and Gamay, were only replanted in 1970, after a gap of some 100 years, as the vineyards in this area had been destroyed by phylloxera. Primarily a region of fruit trees and walnuts, the appellation covers six villages, centred on Glanes, not far from Bretenoux. The wine is light and fruity, with a pleasantly rounded flavour.

Another local curiosity, not sold in any shop or supermarket, is made nearby in the hamlet of Queyssac-les-Vignes. It is a little-known wine called *vin paillé*, not to be confused with the very expensive white *vin de paille* of the Jura. Emmelienne Soursac makes the wine in her farmhouse and is one of the few people to carry on this local tradition. On February 3rd, the feast day of St Blaise, villagers gather at the chapel (named after St Blaise) to drink the sweet red wine and nibble small *beignets*, called *pets-de-nonne*.

To taste *vin paillé*, you must track down Mme Soursac's farm, and ask to be taken into the dark and cobwebby *cave* for a *dégustation*, as the wine comes straight from the barrel. The grapes are picked when very ripe and full of sugar, then left to shrivel on straw mats during the winter. Only in January are they pressed, and the must left to ferment slowly for several months, before the wine is racked off into wooden casks; where it stays until there is a special occasion in the family, or someone comes to buy it. Then Mme Soursac bottles the wine on the spot, with an ancient hand-corking device, and sticks a label on to the recycled bottle at a jaunty angle.

LA PETITE AUBERGE

LASCABANES, MONTCUQ, TEL 65.31.82.51

La Petite Auberge is a working farm, set amid some of the most beautiful scenery of the Quercy. This is where Patrick and Pascale Duler run a delightful country hotel and restaurant as well as raising wild boar, black Gascon pigs and ducks. During quiet times in winter, Patrick and Pascal work as hard as they do in summer, making confits, *bacon, hams and sausages, fruit liqueurs and conserves, to serve to appreciative guests the following spring and summer. The ancient white limestone buildings have been meticulously restored, and a kitchen garden in the valley below provides most of the salads, fruit and vegetables for the restaurant. The experience of eating excellent food – virtually all produced on the farm (including the bread, made from home-grown wheat) –´in such romantic surroundings, is one that is not quickly forgotten.*

POIREAUX BRAISES AUX TRUFFES

Braised Leeks with Truffles

One of the many reclamation projects undertaken by Patrick and Pascal Duler has been the replanting of truffle oaks on their land, and now that they are harvesting their first black truffles, they are keen to find new ways of serving them. This dish combines the sweet blandness of leeks and cream with the powerful aroma of truffle. All it needs is fresh country bread to mop up the juices. (Illustrated below)

SERVES 6
**whites of 12 young, slender leeks
1tbsp butter
100ml/3½fl oz single cream
100g/3½oz black truffles
500ml/16fl oz home-made light meat or chicken stock**

Wash the leeks carefully, and cut into bite-size lengths. In a large pan, melt the butter and braise the leeks over gentle heat for about 30 minutes, turning them over and covering the pan half-way through cooking.

While the leeks are cooking, cut 12 thin slices of truffle, and finely chop the rest into tiny dice. Add these to the cream, together with the truffle juice if using bottled truffles.

When the leeks are cooked, remove them to a serving dish, and keep warm. Deglaze the pan with stock, and bring to the boil. Simmer gently for a few minutes to reduce, then add the cream with the truffle dice, and cook for 5 minutes. Adjust seasoning, and pour the sauce over the leeks, reserving about a spoonful.

Cook the truffle slices gently in a little butter for just a few minutes, then moisten with the spoonful of hot cream sauce. Place the truffle slices on the leeks and cream, and serve.

LE GINDREAU

ST-MEDARD-CATUS, TEL 65.36.22.27

Tucked away in an old schoolhouse in the village of Catus, Alexis and Martine Pélissou run one of Quercy's smartest restaurants. Decorated in neo-classical style, the dining-room is at once elegant and informal, as is the service. Alexis Pélissou is a perfectionist, a chef who scrutinizes every ingredient with his eyes and his nose before it is allowed into his kitchen, rejecting anything that is not up to scratch. Happily, he is well placed for the best the countryside can offer, as Prayssac is nearby, and every Friday the market yields a vanload of local produce: asparagus, strawberries, radishes, flowers, sorrel, herbs, new season's garlic – all freshly gathered that morning. Truffles, foie gras, goats' cheese, Quercy lamb, poultry and eggs are all virtually on the doorstep, as are the red wines of Cahors. The same high standards are maintained in the kitchen: no cutting corners here. While remaining faithful to the notion of terroir, Alexis Pélissou manages to refine and lighten the cooking traditions of Quercy, producing some of the region's most exciting and memorable dishes.

GRATIN D'ASPERGES VERTES AU SABAYON TRUFFE

Gratin of Green Asparagus with Sabayon Sauce and Truffles

Much of the asparagus produced in the Lot is the white or purple variety, but it is green asparagus, with its more pronounced flavour, that Alexis Pélissou chooses as a partner for the pungent aroma of black truffles. The asparagus tips are prepared quite separately from the tougher stems, which benefit from a longer cooking time. Then the dish is dressed with a sabayon. (Illustrated opposite, left)

SERVES 4
2kg/4½lb green asparagus
30g/1oz butter
100g/3½oz Bayonne ham, diced
55g/2oz shallots, finely chopped
1 green garlic shoot
400ml/14fl oz chicken stock

FOR THE SABAYON
3 egg yolks
100ml/3½fl oz champagne or other dry sparkling white wine
15g/½oz truffle, finely chopped
salt and freshly ground black pepper
15g/½oz truffles, thinly sliced, for garnish

Wash and prepare the asparagus, discarding the tough stem bases, then cut off the tips 6cm/2½in from the top, and set aside. Cut the remaining edible part of the stems into 1cm/½in lengths.

Blanch the tips in boiling salted water for 2 minutes, then stop the cooking process by lifting them out, and plunging them straight away into iced water. Drain and set aside.

In a sauté pan, melt the butter, and add the diced ham, shallots and garlic shoot, and cook gently for 5 minutes. Tip the chopped asparagus stems into the pan, and cook very gently, moving them around with a spatula, for a few minutes. Pour in the chicken stock, season with salt and pepper, and bring to the boil. Simmer for 15–20 minutes, uncovered, until the asparagus has formed a kind of ragout.

In another pan, over very gentle heat or in a bain-marie, whisk all of the ingredients for the sabayon, except for the slices of truffle, until the sauce is very smooth and frothy. Check seasoning and keep warm.

Reheat the asparagus tips in a little butter, then, in another pan, gently cook the truffle slices in some butter, and deglaze the pan with some truffle juice if you have any.

To serve, divide the ragout of asparagus stems evenly between four gratin dishes or plates, then arrange the tips on the top of each dish. Pour over the sabayon sauce, and put the dishes under a hot grill to brown. Decorate with slices of truffle.

FONDANT DE POMMES AU CARAMEL MOU

Apple Fondant with Caramel Sauce

A melting concoction of baked apples and caramel, this dessert is a favourite with customers at Le Gindreau. (Illustrated right)

SERVES 8
2kg/4½lb apples, Reinette or Cox
250g/8½oz icing sugar
juice of ½ lemon
vanilla pod
300ml/10fl oz crème fraîche

Peel, core and slice the apples thinly. Mix them with 150g/5½oz of the sugar and the lemon juice, and cook, with the vanilla pod, over brisk heat to evaporate some of the moisture.

Use the remaining sugar to make a soft caramel: first melt 2 tablespoons of the sugar in a heavy saucepan, stirring all the time, until it begins to brown, then add remaining sugar, a spoonful at a time, until it is all dissolved. Allow the caramel to boil steadily to a golden brown, then pour a thin layer over the base of a terrine 20cm/8in long, 7cm/2¾in wide and at least 8cm/3in deep. Cook the remaining caramel with the crème fraîche, leaving it to boil until you have a smooth, slightly thickened sauce. Chill until ready to serve.

Fill the terrine with the cooked apples, place in a bain marie, then cook in a medium oven, 180°C/350°F/gas mark 4, for 1 hour. Cool, then refrigerate for 24 hours before serving.

Unmould the terrine, then, using an electric knife if you have one, slice the apple terrine and place on a serving dish or individual plates. Pour some of the warmed caramel sauce around, decorate with fresh fruit and serve.

TOURAIN A LA TOMATE

Tomato and Garlic Soup

Le tourain, *a kind of instant soup, is popular both in Périgord and Quercy. It can be made in a trice, simply from onions and garlic softened in goose fat, or it can include sorrel, rape or even a piece of* confit; *this ones uses tomatoes. It is best made in summer as sweet, ripe tomatoes are essential for a good flavour; large Marmande tomatoes are ideal if you can find them. (Illustrated left)*

SERVES 4
1tbsp goose fat or oil
2 large onions, sliced
4 garlic cloves, finely chopped
**1kg/2¼lb ripe tomatoes, peeled, deseeded
and chopped**
bay leaf
sprig of thyme
1l/1¾pt water or chicken stock
1 egg
salt and freshly ground black pepper

Heat the fat or oil in a large saucepan, and soften the onions gently, taking care not to let them brown. Add the garlic and the chopped tomatoes, and cook for another 5 minutes. Put in the bay leaf and thyme, add the water or chicken stock, and season with salt and pepper. Bring to the boil, simmer for about 30 minutes, then remove from heat. Adjust the seasoning according to taste.

Beat the egg in a bowl large enough to contain all the soup. Pour the hot soup on to the beaten egg, stirring as you pour, so that the egg, which cooks in the heat, is distributed evenly in the warm soup. Make sure the soup is not too hot, or the eggs will curdle.

Serve immediately, with fresh crusty bread.

TOMATES FARCIES AUX OEUFS DURS

Tomatoes Stuffed with Shallots, Hard-boiled Eggs and Parsley

Marmande tomatoes, sweet and pink, would be perfect for this dish, otherwise find the best you can. Choose those that have ripened on the plants, rather than after picking, as they will have a fuller flavour. (Illustrated opposite)

SERVES 6
**6 large, ripe tomatoes
walnut oil
slice of white bread
2 shallots, chopped
2 garlic cloves, finely chopped
2tbsp mixed chopped fresh herbs –
tarragon, chives, parsley
2 eggs, hard-boiled, peeled and chopped
salt and freshly ground black pepper**

Preheat the oven to 180°C/350°F/gas mark 4. Remove the stalks from the tomatoes, cut a thick slice from the base of each tomato and put to one side, then empty out the juice and seeds. Season the insides with salt, pepper and a little oil, and replace the 'lids'. Place in a buttered dish that neatly takes all of the tomatoes, packing them quite close together, and bake for 20 minutes.

Meanwhile, soften the bread in a little milk, squeeze out the surplus, and shred roughly. Fry the shallots and the garlic lightly in a small amount of walnut oil, then mix with the bread, chopped herbs, chopped hard-boiled eggs and seasoning. Stuff the tomatoes with this mixture and drizzle a little more walnut oil over them. Replace the lids, and return the tomatoes to the oven for another 10 or 15 minutes. Serve with slices of toast rubbed with garlic and walnut oil.

BLETTES AU GRATIN

Gratin of Swiss Chard

Both the coarse, spinach-like leaves and the thick, flat stems of Swiss chard are edible, but it is usually the stems that are considered to have the best flavour. Here, both leaves and stems are served together, with a creamy cheese sauce.

SERVES 4–6
**675g/1½lb Swiss chard
500ml/16fl oz milk
45g/1½oz butter
45g/1½oz flour
pinch of grated nutmeg or mace
85g/3oz gruyère or cantal cheese, grated
salt and freshly ground black pepper**

Wash the chard, then cut the leaves from the stems. Trim the stems, and pull off any tough, stringy bits with a knife. Cut into lengths of about 2.5cm/1in. Cook the leaves with a knob of butter, in a covered saucepan (as you would cook spinach), then drain and chop. Simmer the stems in salted water until tender, about 15 minutes, then drain. Preheat the oven to 180°C/350°F/gas mark 4.

To make the sauce, heat the milk until it boils, then cover and set aside. Melt the butter in another pan, stir in the flour to make a roux, cook for 2–3 minutes, then add the milk, stirring vigorously to prevent lumps from forming. Bring back to the boil, simmer for 2–3 minutes, still stirring, then add the nutmeg and all but about 2 tablespoons of the cheese. Season to taste with salt and pepper.

Arrange a layer of chopped leaves in a gratin dish, cover with the stems, and pour the sauce over. Strew with grated cheese and bake for 20–30 minutes, or until the top is golden brown in colour.

ESTOUFFADE

Ragout of Potatoes and Ceps

Estouffade, or estouffat, is usually a dish of slowly cooked meat, rather like a daube. In the village of Thégra, not far from Saint-Céré, a variation of the traditional estouffade is made with potatoes and ceps, gently cooked in duck fat and sprinkled with a persillade. The dish can be made with brown-cap cultivated mushrooms instead, although the flavour will not be quite so rich.

SERVES 4
**675g/1½lb potatoes, peeled and very thinly sliced
450g/1lb fresh ceps
2tbsp goose or duck fat
1tbsp oil
2 garlic cloves, finely chopped
2tbsp finely chopped parsley
salt and freshly ground black pepper**

Dry the potato slices with a clean tea-towel. In a large frying pan, heat the fat and oil, and then add the potatoes. Stir around, so that all of the slices are coated with fat, and cook over medium heat for 30 minutes, shaking the pan from time to time to ensure that they don't stick and start to burn, and turning them over as they cook.

While they are cooking, wipe the ceps with a damp cloth, only washing them if absolutely necessary. Trim the stems, and cut into rounds. Slice the caps. Add the ceps to the pan, turning them over with a spatula to mix them with the potatoes. Season with salt and pepper, cover and cook for about another 15 minutes. Sprinkle with garlic and parsley, cook for another 5 minutes and serve, perhaps as an accompaniment to *confit* or roast meat.

CROUTE AUX CHAMPIGNONS

Mushroom Tart

This rich mushroom tart is one of the speciali-ties of Patrick Duler, chef-patron at La Petite Auberge, where it is served in front of a wood fire in winter. It is substantial enough to form the main dish of a light supper or lunch, but here it is presented as a starter.

SERVES 6–8 AS A STARTER
FOR THE PASTRY
200g/7oz plain flour
85g/3oz cold butter, cut into small cubes
50ml/3tbsp iced water
butter, for greasing

FOR THE FILLING
800g/1¾lb button mushrooms
3tbsp chicken stock
85g/3oz butter or 2tbsp duck fat
85g/3oz flour
2 eggs, beaten
2 heaped tbsp crème fraîche
25g/¾oz gruyère cheese, grated
salt and freshly ground black pepper

To make the pastry, put the flour and a large pinch of salt in a bowl, then add the butter, and work it into the flour with your fingers, until it reaches the consistency of bread-crumbs. Add the cold water and knead lightly. Wrap in film and chill for 2 hours. Preheat the oven to 250°C/475°F/gas mark 9, and roll out the pastry. Grease a 25.5cm/10in tart tin, and line with the pastry. Prick the bottom all over with a fork, and put in the hot oven for 8 min-utes. Remove and set aside.

To make the filling, cut off the mushroom stalks, and carefully wash the mushrooms to remove all grit and soil. Slice them very thinly. Place in a large saucepan with the chicken stock and 2 tablespoons of water, cover tightly, bring to the boil, and simmer for 15 minutes, so that the mushrooms release their liquid into the stock. Preheat the oven again to 250°C/475°F/gas mark 9.

Remove the mushrooms with a slotted spoon, and press lightly in a colander to remove excess liquid. Reserve the stock. Melt the butter or goose fat in a sauté pan over gentle heat, add the flour and stir with a wooden spoon. Season with salt and pepper. As soon as the roux thickens, start adding the stock little by little, stirring constantly until the sauce is smooth and all the stock has been used up. If there is not enough stock, add a little milk. Continue to cook for 2 or 3 minutes, then turn off the heat. Add the mushrooms, still stirring, then the beaten eggs and the crème fraîche. Blend thoroughly, pour into the pastry case, and sprinkle with grated cheese. Bake in the hot oven for 20 minutes. Serve warm.

CHOU FARCI

Stuffed Cabbage with Chestnuts

There are almost as many recipes for chou farci *as there are cooks in France, the* farce, *or stuff-ing, varying according to what is available, and to individual preference.*

In regions such as La Châtaignerie, in the north-east part of the Quercy, chestnuts were once the staple food of pigs as well as people. In the past, they were dried in a small outhouse called a secadou *in order to preserve them through the winter, whereas now they can be bought ready cooked and peeled, in cans or vacuum-packed, which saves on the time-consuming task of removing their skins.*

Sausagemeat in France is made from pure pork, not padded out with cereal and other ingredients as it is in Britain, and it tastes much better as a result. Good butchers, even in Britain, should be able to supply this quality; otherwise buy belly pork and mince it in the food processor. (Illustrated opposite).

SERVES 4–6
1 Savoy-type cabbage

FOR THE STUFFING
85g/3oz celeriac, peeled and diced
2 shallots, finely chopped
1 garlic clove, chopped
1tbsp butter or goose fat
450g/1lb chestnuts, blanched and peeled
55g/2oz breadcrumbs
1 dessert apple, peeled and diced
200g/7oz good quality sausagemeat
85g/3oz smoked streaky bacon, diced
100g/3½oz *jambon de campagne*
2 eggs, beaten
2tbsp chopped parsley and thyme
salt and freshly ground black pepper

FOR THE BOUILLON
1tbsp goose fat
bouquet garni
1 carrot, chopped
1 onion, chopped
1 glass white wine

Preheat the oven to 160°C/325°F/gas mark 4. Braise the celeriac cubes in a buttered baking dish in the oven for about 25 minutes. Meanwhile, gently soften the shallots and garlic in half the remaining butter in a saucepan over a low heat.

Trim the cabbage, removing any tough outer leaves. Put the whole cabbage in a large pan of boiling water, and simmer for about 10 minutes, to soften the leaves slightly; then take it out and leave to drain upside-down.

In a large basin, mix all of the stuffing ingredients, season with salt and pepper and knead together. Lay out a piece of muslin (make sure it is large enough to wrap the cabbage in) on a table, and place the drained cabbage, stalk down, on it. Starting at the outside, gently pull back the leaves so that they lie almost flat, and place a spoonful of stuffing on each leaf, unfolding them one by one, until all the mixture has been used up.

Gather up the muslin, pull it tightly around the cabbage so that it becomes almost round again, and tie with string.

Melt a spoonful of butter or goose fat in a saucepan large enough to hold the cabbage, and place the cabbage inside. Tuck in the bouquet garni, add the chopped carrot and onion around, and moisten with the white wine and 500ml/16fl oz water; cover and cook over a gentle heat 2–3 hours. To serve, remove the muslin, place the cabbage on a large dish, and cut it into even slices, like a pudding.

Serve the wedges with a fresh tomato sauce, or mustard and pickled *cornichons*.

LAPIN AUX PRUNEAUX

Rabbit with Prunes

Rabbits are a familar sight in the farmyards or basse-cours of Quercy, usually ranged in cages near the kitchen door. Obligingly keen to multiply, and quick to put on weight, they are fed on vegetable scraps and grain, and are soon ready for the pot.

SERVES 4
12 fat prunes
1 glass red wine, combined with equal
quantity of water
1 rabbit, jointed
1tbsp seasoned flour
1tbsp goose fat
1 onion, chopped
1 thick slice of bacon, diced
pinch of dried thyme
bay leaf

Soak the prunes in wine and water for 2–3 hours, so that they swell up.

Preheat the oven to 160°C/325°F/gas mark 3. Coat the rabbit pieces in seasoned flour, and fry them in the goose fat, turning over as they take on colour, until nicely browned. Remove them from the pan and place in an ovenproof casserole dish with a lid.

Lower heat, and tip the chopped onion and diced bacon into the fat. Cook for about 5 minutes, until softened and starting to colour. Empty the contents of the pan into the casserole, tucking the onions and bacon around the pieces of rabbit. Remove the prunes from the wine, and add them to the casserole as well. Use the wine to deglaze the frying pan, and pour this over the rabbit. Sprinkle with thyme, add the bay leaf, and cover the casserole tightly. Cook in the oven for about 2 hours.

TOURTIERE AU SALSIFIS

Chicken Pie with Salsify

Tourtières are fairly shallow, cast-iron cooking pots, with three legs; the lid is shaped so that hot embers from the fire could be piled on it, and the contents would be heated from both below and above – feu dessous, feu dessus. A pie dish or moule à manqué in a modern oven does more or less the same job.

The pastry is a rich pâte brisée *made with pork fat or lard. Do not be tempted to substitute industrially made lard: if you cannot find butcher's lard, use butter instead. In the absence of fresh salsify, it can be bought in a tin, ready cooked, or you could use peeled Jerusalem artichokes. (Illustrated opposite)*

SERVES 6
FOR THE PASTRY
225g/8oz rendered pork fat (saindoux)
450g/1lb flour
2 eggs, beaten

FOR THE FILLING
450g/1lb fresh salsify or 1 x 400g/14oz can
cooked salsify
1tbsp goose fat
2 thick slices smoked bacon, diced
8 shallots
2 carrots or small turnips, peeled and diced
1 free-range chicken, weighing about
1.35kg/3lb, jointed
150ml/5fl oz dry white wine
squeeze of lemon juice
bouquet garni
1 heaped tbsp plain flour
2tbsp crème fraîche
yolks of 2 eggs
1tbsp each chopped garlic, parsley, chives

If using fresh salsify, peel the roots using a stainless steel knife, and put the pieces into water with a little vinegar or lemon juice added to prevent discoloration. Cut each root into lengths of about 2.5cm/1in.

In a large sauté pan or casserole, heat the goose fat and add the bacon, the peeled whole shallots and carrots or turnips. Cook gently for about 10 minutes, then remove with a slotted spoon, and set aside. Brown the chicken pieces in the hot fat, turning several times; then take these out of the pan while you deglaze with the white wine, scraping all of the brown bits from the bottom of the pan.

Put the chicken pieces, bacon and vegetables (including the salsify, if using fresh), back into the pan with the wine, add the lemon juice, 600ml/21fl oz water, bouquet garni and seasoning; cover the pan and simmer for 30 minutes.

At the end of the cooking time, strain the stock and chill; the fat will rise to the surface and later most of it will be skimmed away. Skin the chicken pieces, discard gristle and bones, and cut the meat into chunks. Set aside, with the vegetables, in a covered bowl.

Skim a tablespoon of fat off the cooled stock, and put in a saucepan over gentle heat. Stir in flour to make a roux. (Skim the remaining fat off the stock and discard.) When the flour is well blended with the fat, add remaining stock (there should be about 700ml/1¼pt). Simmer for 5 minutes, then stir in the crème fraîche.

In a bowl, beat the egg yolks, and pour the hot sauce over the eggs, whisking constantly, so that it thickens. Check seasoning, add the herbs, and pour 300ml/10fl oz of the sauce over vegetables and chicken. The rest can be reheated and served with the cooked *tourtière*.

If using canned salsify, drain it well and add it now. At this stage, the filling can be left to cool and refrigerated overnight.

To make the pastry case, leave the pork fat at room temperature to soften for an hour, then sift the flour and a little salt into a bowl, and make a hollow in the centre. Pour the beaten eggs into the hollow. Work the eggs and softened lard into the flour with your fingertips, as lightly and quickly as possible. Form the pastry into a ball, adding a little water only if necessary, and leave to rest for at least an hour, wrapped in a tea-towel, at room temperature.

When ready to bake the pie, preheat the oven to 220°C/425°F/gas mark 7. Divide the pastry into two parts, one slightly larger than the other, and roll out the larger one first. The crust is baked blind. Use the larger round of pastry to line a buttered 23cm/9in pie dish at least 5cm/2in deep, or a *moule à manqué.* Roll out the remaining pastry and lay a twisted tea-towel turban-like inside the pie crust. Cover with the pastry lid. Pinch together the pastry at

intervals around the edge but only do this loosely, as you will need to remove the crust later to put in the filling. Make a small hole in the centre of the lid, and place a chimney of rolled paper through the hole. Bake for 30–40 minutes, or until nicely browned.

Reheat the filling if necessary, and gently prise off the top of the pastry case. Remove the tea-towel. Spoon the filling inside, replace the pastry lid, and serve, with any extra sauce.

CARRE D'AGNEAU FERMIER DU QUERCY EN CROUTE DE NOIX

Cutlets of Quercy Lamb in a Walnut Crust

This recipe is the invention of Gilles Marre, chef-patron of Le Balandre in Cahors, one of Quercy's finest restaurants. Using tender lamb from the limestone causses, and locally grown walnuts, he skilfully combines two Quercy products in this simple but effective dish.

SERVES 4
1 egg
85g/3oz walnuts, finely chopped
2 pieces best end of neck of lamb, with 6 ribs in each, 'French trimmed', skin and fat removed
salt and freshly ground black pepper
oil, for frying
250ml/8fl oz well-flavoured lamb stock

TO SERVE
an assortment of young seasonal vegetables: carrots, turnips, courgettes, new potatoes, cut into pieces of similar size and shape
butter, for greasing

Preheat the oven to 200°C/400°F/gas mark 6.

Beat the egg in a shallow bowl, and season with salt and pepper. Spread the chopped nuts on a plate. Dip the pieces of meat into the egg, coating them all over, then roll over the walnuts, pressing down well so that they stick to the surface of the meat.

Heat a little oil in a frying pan and brown the meat, one piece at a time, turning over so that all sides come into contact with the hot fat, and form a crisp crust. When browned all over,

transfer to an oven-proof dish, and continue to cook in the oven; allow 20 minutes for rare lamb and 30 minutes for medium-cooked lamb. Meanwhile, cook the vegetables separately in salted boiling water, drain and glaze by tossing in butter.

Just before serving, set the meat on a carving board, rib upwards, and cut down between the ribs. Arrange the slices of meat on a serving dish with the vegetables, and keep warm until ready to serve.

In the pan in which the meat has been browned, heat the lamb stock, scraping all of the brown bits into the liquid. Simmer until the sauce is sufficiently concentrated, skim off the fat, check the seasoning and serve with the lamb and vegetables.

RAGOUT D'ASPERGES

Braised Shoulder of Veal with Asparagus

Mme Delpech is not a great lover of asparagus, probably because she and her family grow it commercially at their farm near Dausse, in the Lot valley. But this family recipe, in which asparagus is braised with veal and mushrooms, is always in demand.

SERVES 6–8
450g/1lb asparagus
2tbsp goose fat, oil or butter
1 large onion, chopped
3 garlic cloves
1.35kg/3lb shoulder of veal, boned weight
2tbsp seasoned flour
1 glass white wine
10fl oz/300ml veal stock
bay leaf
2 tomatoes, peeled and chopped
450g/1lb brown cap mushroom
30g/1oz butter
2tbsp chopped parsley
2 egg yolks
4 generous tbsp thick cream

Peel and trim the asparagus, discarding the tough, inedible base of each stem, and cut into pieces about 2cm/¾in long; keep the tips whole and reserve. Heat the fat in a flameproof casserole, and gently fry the onion, garlic and asparagus stems. With a slotted spoon, remove vegetables and set aside.

Cut the meat into fairly large chunks, coat with seasoned flour, and add to the pan, turning over several times so that the pieces are brown on all sides. Pour in the white wine, scrape the sides and bottom of the pan to loosen any bits which have stuck, and stir these into the liquid. Add the stock, bay leaf and chopped tomatoes, replace vegetables and cover the pan, then simmer very gently or cook in the oven at 150°C/300°F/gas mark 2 for about an hour, or until the meat is tender.

When the meat is almost cooked, slice the mushrooms and fry them in butter, then sprinkle with chopped parsley and add to the ragout for the last 10 minutes of cooking. If the sauce is too liquid, remove the meat to a serving dish, cover and keep warm while you reduce the liquid by boiling in a saucepan. Beat the egg yolks and cream together, and blend with the hot sauce. Do not let the sauce boil again once the eggs have been added. Blanch the asparagus tips in boiling water for 4–5 minutes, drain and arrange over the top of the ragout.

PASTIS QUERCYNOIS

Apple Pie with Filo Pastry

Not to be confused with the anis-flavoured aperitif, pastis *is a speciality of Quercy. The finished gâteau resembles an overblown rose, the 'petals' made of transparent sheets of filo-type pastry, glazed golden brown with a syrup of eau-de-vie, sugar and water.*

Making the pastry is a time-consuming task, requiring skill and patience. You need to allow at least five hours, as the dough must rest for three hours first. Mme Boussou, who used to run a restaurant on the banks of the Lot, near Cahors, remembers her mother placing a quilt over the dough to keep it warm while it rested. The dough was then pulled out from the centre, and stretched out until it covered the surface of an old sheet dusted with flour, placed over a very large kitchen table.

This version uses ready-made filo pastry, an acceptable substitute. (Illustrated right)

SERVES **6**
150ml/5fl oz flavourless cooking oil
5tbsp eau-de-vie or rum
1 x 275g/9½oz packet of filo pastry
115g/4oz sugar
3 tart eating apples, peeled and thinly sliced
syrup made from 3tbsp sugar, 2tbsp hot
water and 1tbsp eau-de-vie

Preheat the oven to 190°C/375°F/gas mark 5.

Generously oil a 24cm/9½in *moule à manqué* or deep flan tin. In a small dish, mix together the remaining oil and the eau-de-vie or rum.

Take 2 sheets of filo pastry, and use them to line the tin, laying them at right angles to each other. Leave any extra pastry hanging out over the edges of the tin. Sprinkle with oil and eau-de-vie, then dust with sugar.

The aim when assembling the pie is to build up the leaves of pastry, radiating from the centre around the dish, so that they overlap each other at the edges, rather like the petals of a flower. Begin by loosely placing a sheet of pastry with one corner over the centre of the tin, and the opposite corner hanging out over the side. Sprinkle with oil and eau-de-vie, then with sugar, then cover with another sheet of pastry, overlapping the previous one, and continue working around the tin, sprinkling each layer with oil, eau-de-vie and sugar. Do not press down, as the layers should have plenty of air between the crinkly folds.

When the base is entirely covered by 3 layers of pastry, add a layer of apple slices, and sprinkle with oil, eau-de-vie and sugar. Continue to build up the pie with a layer of apples after every 2 layers of pastry, and sprinkling each layer, until all are used up. The triangular, overhanging flaps of pastry should be fairly evenly distributed around the edge of the tin, and can now be folded back roughly towards

the centre, leaving plenty of air between them, creating a crumpled surface that will become crisp with baking. Sprinkle the surface with the remaining oil, eau-de-vie and sugar, and bake for 30 minutes, then remove from the oven, and sprinkle with the syrup of eau-de-vie, sugar and water. Return to the oven for another 5 minutes.

Serve warm, dusted with icing sugar.

CONFITURE DE TOMATES VERTES

Green Tomato Jam

Traditionally made throughout the Dordogne, green tomato jam tastes surprisingly of melons. It is produced at the Favol's factory, at Villeneuve-sur-Lot. (Illustrated opposite).

450g/1lb green tomatoes
450g/1lb sugar
1 lemon

Cut the tomatoes into small pieces, add the sugar, and leave overnight in a bowl, so that the sugar dissolves. The next day, cut the lemon into very fine slices, add it to the tomatoes and bring the mixture to the boil in a pan; stir from time to time to make sure the sugar is completely dissolved before the jam boils.

Simmer until the tomatoes are tender, and the jam forms a skin when tested on a cold saucer, then pot up in jars the normal way.

MASSEPAIN

Light Sponge Cake with Orange Flower Water

The name massepain *suggests a kind of almond cake, or marzipan, but this sponge contains no almonds. (Illustrated opposite)*

SERVES 6–8
6 eggs, separated
200g/7oz caster sugar
a few drops of vanilla essence
1 scant tsp of orange flower water
butter, for greasing
200g/7oz plain flour

Preheat the oven to 160°C/325°F/gas mark 3. Whisk the egg yolks with the sugar until they are pale and creamy. Add the orange flower water and vanilla essence, then sift the flour into the mixture, and fold in. In another bowl, whisk the egg whites until stiff, then fold these gently into the flour, yolks and sugar. Butter a 20cm/8in cake tin generously, then carefully pour in the mixture, and bake in the oven for 40 minutes; do not be tempted to open the oven door before the time is up. During baking, it will rise beautifully and become golden brown, but will sink slightly as it cools, forming a pleasantly wrinkled surface.

Unmould, sprinkle with icing sugar, and serve warm or cold.

SABLES AUX PRUNEAUX

Rich Pastry Tartlets Filled with Prune Purée

Crème de pruneaux – *prune purée – can be bought in jars in the Agenais, but it is easy enough to make. It can also be used to make delicious instant desserts, blended with crème fraîche or fromage frais. (Illustrated opposite)*

MAKES 9 TARTLETS
225g/8oz plain flour
½ tbsp salt
115g/4oz cold butter
85g/3oz sugar
few drops vanilla essence
4 egg yolks plus 1 whole egg
about 285g/10oz *crème de pruneaux*

FOR THE CREME DE PRUNEAUX
225g/8oz stoned prunes
3tbsp lemon juice
225g/8oz jam sugar, with pectin

To make the *crème de pruneaux*, first soak prunes in 150ml/5fl oz water and the lemon juice for 2 hours, then cook the prunes in this liquid until soft. Remove the prunes with a slotted spoon, and allow the juice to cool, then stir in the sugar, and heat slowly, stirring until all the sugar is dissolved, and not allowing the syrup to boil. Purée the prunes and syrup together in a blender, return to the pan, and boil for 2 minutes, stirring continuously. Pour into clean glass jars and seal with lids. Store in a cool place.

To make the tartlets, sift flour and salt into a mixing bowl, and using the coarse side on a cheese grater, grate the butter into the flour. With the tips of your fingers, quickly rub the fat into the flour, until the mixture looks like breadcrumbs. Sprinkle in the sugar and vanilla essence, then make a well in the mixture, and add the egg yolks. Gather the mixture together with your fingers, and combine the ingredients to make an even dough, kneading lightly if necessary. Chill for 30 minutes or more.

Preheat the oven to 180°C/350°F/gas mark 4. Divide the pastry in two, and roll out half to about 30 x 30cm/12 x 12in. To make this process easier (as the pastry has a tendency to stick), roll it between 2 sheets of film, or floured waxed paper, loosening the paper from time to time. Using a circular cutter about 9cm/3½in in diameter, cut out 9 rounds, and lay these on a buttered baking sheet. Place a generous teaspoon of prune purée in the centre of each. Beat the remaining whole egg, and brush a circle of egg around the edges of the tartlets. Roll out the rest of the pastry, and make lattice tops for the tarts, or cut more rounds to make solid lids. Brush the pastry lids with beaten egg, and bake the tartlets for 15–20 minutes, or until golden brown. Serve warm or cold, on their own or with vanilla ice-cream or whipped cream.

ABOVE *A solitary swan makes its way serenely
across the Dordogne river, beneath
the bridge at Bergerac.*
RIGHT *The morning's catch of bleak (*les ablettes*),
small river fish about the size of sardines, which
are used to make* la friture de la Dordogne.
FAR RIGHT *Now semi-retired, 'The Pelican', as he is
known, is one of the most famous of
Dordogne fishermen. In the past he sold fish from
his riverside home, and supplied
local restaurants with pike, zander, bream,
perch and barbel.*

BERGERAC AND THE RIVER

From its source in the Mont Dore region of the Massif Central, the young river Dordogne bubbles and cascades through narrow gorges, on its way towards the first of the vast hydro-electric dams at Bort les Orgues; in middle age, between Bretenoux and Bergerac, it meanders gracefully through a dream-like valley of fertile fields and honey-coloured villages; then, as an old river, it slowly makes its way through flat alluvial plains, to its final merging with the sea in the Gironde. It is a journey of some 500 kilometres, and includes some of the loveliest pastoral landscapes in the world.

For spectacular scenery, it is the middle section that is outstanding. Here, in summer, the fields burst into a colourful patchwork of strip cultivation, punctuated by lines of poplar trees and walnut groves. Cutting steep cliffs into the limestone, the river loops around lazily, forming wide *cingles*, and providing convenient cliff-top sites for lofty castles, some ruined, some restored, around which cling stone-roofed cottages. It is all unbelievably picturesque.

Towards the old port of Bergerac, the plain broadens out still further to embrace the gently undulating vineyards of the Bergeraçois, which thrive in the mild climate and fertile soils of the region, and orchards intersperse the southern slopes of vines.

RIVER TRAFFIC

In the days before railway tracks were laid, and when roads were virtually impassable in winter, the river really was the main artery of the area, linking the easterly uplands of the Massif Central with the Atlantic port of Bordeaux. The Dordogne teemed with traffic. Boats plied their way up and down the river, carrying timber, wine and paper from the interior of France to the seaports, and bringing salt, dried and salted sea-fish, sugar and rum back to the people of the Quercy, Limousin and Auvergne. The Bordelais was especially dependent on the river for its supplies of timber, used not only for vine stakes, but also for making barrels.

Basic foodstuffs such as salt and sugar were transported by river to the inland areas of Périgord and Quercy, as well as rum from the tropics, which became a favourite ingredient in the preparation of cakes and desserts. Traversing Quercy, Périgord and the Bordelais, the river allowed the exchange not only of goods, but also of ideas and recipes.

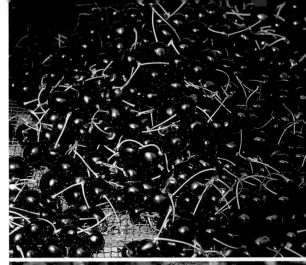

The import of salted and dried fish – *morue* and *stockfisch* – from northern seas relieved the dullness of *jours maigres* for Catholics who had no direct access to fresh sea-fish, and gave rise to dozens of regional dishes, the most famous being *gâteau de morue*, a creamy gratin made of salt cod with potato purée, eggs and walnut oil (see page 115). With a little imagination, the same versatile ingredients could be used in a different way, to make a warm salad of potato and salt cod with hard-boiled eggs, or crisp round fritters called *beignets* (see page 110). It is not difficult to understand why salt cod became so popular, and has remained so, even though refrigeration and efficient transport mean that this ancient method of preservation is no longer necessary.

River journeys were long and hazardous: it could take up to three weeks to travel from Souillac to Libourne (a journey which today would take less than three hours) but the rewards were great, and river ports such as Bergerac, Mauzac and Lalinde thrived, with boat-builders, coopers, merchants and hotel-keepers all benefitting from the passing traffic. Along the banks of the Dordogne, these little ports all had their stone quays, called *peyrats*, where the *gabariers* could tie up their boats to unload. The advent of the railways and the building of bridges in the late nineteenth century heralded the death of the old river trade; but new businesses have taken its place, with restaurant and café tables lining the waterside in these tiny ports and busy towns along the river's length.

So the river remains a life force of the region, attracting visitors in their thousands, and it is impossible to imagine this part of France without the soothing and mesmeric effect of its constant flow of water.

THE BERGERACOIS

Bergerac is a fine, prosperous town, with an old quarter full of narrow medieval streets, and brick and timber-framed houses around the Place du Docteur Cayla and the Place de la Myrpe. The Maison du Vin, housed in the delightful Clôtre des Recollets, and the Museum of Wine, Boating and Cooperage, are all located in this area. A statue of Cyrano de Bergerac stands in the same square, despite the fact that the seventeenth-century philosopher who was the inspiration for Rostand's play was in no way linked to this town. A stone's throw away is the old port, where the *gabares* (river barges) used to tie up, in order to drop off their cargo and pick up barrels of wine for export.

Around Bergerac, the valley of the Dordogne becomes very wide. The Bergeraçois, as the region is known, enjoys a mild climate which favours all kinds of meridional crops: cherries, plums, pears, peaches and nectarines. Often, fruit trees are planted among the vines, either dotted around or in rows between the vineyards, adding yet more variety to the gently undulating countryside. This land is a gardener's paradise, and everywhere there are neat plots of vegetables packed with beans and peas, salsify and sorrel, artichokes and spinach.

Surplus produce is sold on Saturday mornings, around the Gothic church of Notre Dame in Bergerac. There is also a market on Wednesdays specializing in flowers and plants, but Saturday is the day for food. To get the pick of the produce you must arrive early, perhaps

Translucent red cherries, with their tang of sour-sweetness; crisp radishes and orange-fleshed Charentais melons signal the passage from spring to summer in the market at Bergerac, held around the church.

Hand-made willow baskets are a sideline for some stallholders, woven on quiet winter days when there is little to do in the garden. Apart from the business of buying and selling, market day is also the time for enjoying a chat with friends, or simply standing back to watch the world go by. Pink-blotched apricots have a heady scent.

Dark green baby courgettes, each with their yellow flowers attached, are as tempting to a cook as the sight and smell of fresh herbs: basil, fennel and thyme nestle among bunches of sorrel and chard.

just stopping briefly on the way to sample the buttery, warm croissants from the Pâtisserie Rosier, in the Rue de la Résistance. They are quite simply the best in town. Then a quick tour of the market reveals dozens of *petits producteurs* selling their wares; in spring, they have bunches of pink radishes, their perky roots waving in the air, watercress of a particularly brilliant green, spring onions and winter salads. The cheese stall has *chèvre frais* with wrinkled skins, carefully displayed in mini-pyramids; Saint-Nectaire *fermier*; Cantal and a local *tomme fermier*, made from cows' milk. The enthusiasm for all this fresh food is palpable; an old lady is almost jumping up and down with delight at the thought of a favourite way of serving fresh goats' cheese with honey. Several stalls have only a couple of fat ducks and a few dozen eggs to sell, for these are genuine farm products. The first asparagus of the season is also on show, with pink and purple tips, together with asparagus roots for the garden, looking like bunches of old rope.

VIN DE PECHE

Peach leaves, as well as the actual fruit, have the miraculous capacity to transfer their heady perfume and flavour to alcohol, if left to macerate for a while. For best results, pick the leaves just after the fruit has ripened. You will need colourless, flavourless eau-de-vie, which is sold especially for preserving fruit and making liqueurs. If it is not already diluted to the correct strength, water it down to 45° or 50°. For every 100 peach leaves, take 1 glass of eau-de-vie, 20 lumps of sugar, and 1l/1¾pt of rosé wine. Place all of the ingredients in a clean bottle or jar, seal well, and leave in a cool, dark place for ten days. The vin de pêche should then be filtered, transferred to clean bottles, and left for a month or so for the flavour to develop. Served chilled, it makes a delicious and refreshing aperitif.

RIGHT Picking peaches near Eymet, during the month of June. Both yellow and white-fleshed peaches are grown in the Bergeraçois, the white varieties usually fetching higher prices due to their superior flavour. (Peaches are extremely delicate, and each fruit must be laid carefully in the box to avoid bruising.)

RIGHT A picturesque group of agricultural buildings, with barns and dairies, pigsties and hen-houses, tobacco-drying sheds and farm-workers' cottages around the central courtyard. Constructed of golden stone, these long low buildings are typical of the region.

BAKER
GILBERT BARDONE

Bread cannot be more wholesome than this. The handwritten sign on Gilbert Bardone's market stall proclaims 'pain biologique, garanti sans levure', while the brown loaves and paper bags echo the theme of healthy living. The baker's smiling face beckons, and soon the casual passer-by is caught up in animated conversation, for Gilbert Bardone loves to talk, especially about bread.

He uses no yeast, he explains, but only a sourdough starter to make the dough rise, because during yeast-activated fermentation, an enzyme called phytase develops, and renders beneficial minerals in flour unassimilable. So it is only by eating pain au levain *that we can absorb all of the valuable calcium, magnesium and iron contained in wholewheat flour. Certainly, he looks in the best of health – can this be the reason?*

All of his bread is made from freshly milled, stoneground, organic flour, and although he bakes fewer than 100 loaves a day, there is always a wide choice of different grains: 100% wholemeal, rye, five-cereal (wheat, oats, barley, buckwheat and rye), brioche, as well as special seasonal breads – with walnuts, raisins, olives or sesame seeds. Although at its best when fresh, it keeps moist for much longer than yeast-risen bread, so regular customers stock up for the week.

Gilbert Bardone's bread can be found at Périgueux market on Wednesday, Bergerac on Saturday, and Le Bugue on Tuesday.

FISHING THE FRESH WATER
ABOVE BERGERAC

FRESHWATER FISH

*Zander or pike-perch (*le sandre*); roach
(*le gardon*); carp (*la carpe*) and bream (*la brème*),
are all caught in the Dordogne, and
occasionally served in local restaurants. Once an
important part of the diet of people living close
to the river, the popularity of freshwater
fish is declining. But, despite its diminished
commercial importance, fishing holds many
attractions for the amateur. Apart from the
species shown above, pike, eel and barbel are
landed with great frequency, as well as the
occasional brown trout or grayling.
Professional fishermen use a variety of nets
and traps, rather than a rod and line, ranging
from* la nasse, *or* la bourgne *as it is known locally
- a flask-shaped device woven from willow - to*
l'épervier, *a weighted net that is cast across the
river, in which small fry such as bleak and
gudgeon become entangled as they try to pass.*

Whereas in the past the river provided a vital transport link with the outside world and was central to the culture and prosperity of the whole Dordogne region, today the valley attracts a huge influx of tourists in summer; the brightly coloured canoes and kayaks of holiday-makers, and the occasional fisherman's barque, are all that remain of river traffic. Most of these visitors come to enjoy the river setting, and many hope to eat freshly caught fish from the river at a small auberge or a waterside restaurant. Such places are few and far between, but a handful of small, simple restaurants still flourish, serving *la soupe de poissons*, made from freshwater fish, as well as pike, eel, shad and zander, in unpretentious surroundings.

At the turn of the century, fishing provided an income for a substantial part of the riverside population; in the tiny village of Beynac there were more than 20 full-time fishermen. Today, there are fewer than 20 professional fishermen on the entire river above Bergerac, and most of these do other work, with fishing providing only about a third of their income.

The reasons for this are many. For a start, fishing is hard work and does not bring in a large income, and the young seem less willing to accept a lower standard of living for the sake of working in constant contact with nature, with all of its pleasures and pains. Fishing laws are stricter now than in the past, when each fisherman was allowed three *compagnons*, who also had the right to catch and sell fish. Furthermore, there are fewer fish.

Only fifteen years ago, freshwater fish – pike, carp, perch, gudgeon, bleak – were sold by Père Laborderie at the market at Sarlat, in willow baskets covered with damp sacking to keep them fresh. After the market, the fisherman would take to the hills, delivering what remained to regular customers in outlying villages, who were keen to take whatever was on offer. But, although those days are gone, real enthusiasts can still find such delicacies if they know where to look.

In the Hôtel-Restaurant Cayre, a two-star Logis on the banks of the Dordogne at Rouffilhac, the tradition of fishing and eating fish lives on. Jean-Louis Cayre, a professional fisherman, started this restaurant 25 years ago, and now it is run by his son Jean-Noël and grandson Eric. Fishing is a fairly unpredictable occupation, and must be combined with other activities to provide a viable income, and so it seemed obvious that the family should work together. By running a fish restaurant, there is a guaranteed market for the fish that Jean-Louis catches, while at the same time regular customers understand that supplies are seasonal and are happy to eat whatever the day's catch brings. There may be bleak for *la friture de la Dordogne* (see page 108), pike for *brochet farci maison* (see page 114), or eel for a *matelote* with red wine (see page 115). On Sundays, Eric cooks zander with girolle mushrooms, ingredients permitting, and occasionally during the summer there is brown river trout, a rare treat.

A *matelote* of eel is also one of the specialities at the Hôtel des Pêcheurs, at Badefols-sur-Dordogne, but here they prefer to cook it with white wine, rather than red. Also on the menu are grilled carp fillets; perch fillets with *sauce verte*; pike and zander. Both the dining-room and terrace have views of the river, which virtually laps around the foot of the building.

Maurice Jardel, a swarthy hulk of a man, with a ready smile and a generous heart, is one of the few remaining professional fishermen in the department of the Dordogne. Despite the high taxes he has to pay for the privilege, and the cost of buying and maintaining his boat, tackle and *engins* – the term used to describe various kinds of fish trap – he remains passionate about fishing, and manages to make ends meet by being part of the family business. His son Bruno, as well as being a farmer, owns the Hotel-Restaurant du Pont at Groléjac (see pages 108–9), and so that is where Maurice takes his catch. Here you can sample *soupe de poissons*, made from bony fish like barbel and bream; *friture de la Dordogne*; and *filet de sandre*, freshly caught that morning from the river which flows just a stone's throw away from the hotel. From mid-April to mid-June during the closed season, *le repos*, there is little or no fishing but plenty of work to be done in the fields, planting tobacco and maize, while the tourist season coincides neatly with an abundance of summer fish.

Maurice Jardel learned the secrets of river fishing from his grandfather – how to observe the water height and temperature, the phases of the moon, the habits of different fish, and how to know which net or trap to use, and when – and he looks forward to the day when he can take his grandson out fishing. Six-year-old Florian already has his own boat, ready for that day. It is Maurice's great hope that the family tradition will continue, and '*la jeunesse reprendra le flambeau*' – the next generation will carry the torch.

BELOW For the amateur fisherman, nothing can beat a peaceful afternoon on the riverbank, rod at the ready. Fishing permits can be purchased from bars, tabacs and fishing shops, and details of regulations concerning open and closed seasons, and other fishing laws, can be obtained from the regional fishing association, La Fédération Départementale des Associations Agrées de Pêche et de Pisciculture, in Périgueux. There are, for example, two categories of river - those containing trout and those with no trout, and different rules apply to each. Certain species are protected, too. The fishing of sturgeon is banned throughout France, and salmon fishing is not allowed in the Dordogne at present.

SAVING THE SALMON

Not only pike, eel and zander, but shad, seatrout, sturgeon and salmon were all once abundant in the waters of the Dordogne, but the building of the dams at Mauzac and Bergerac in the nineteenth century had a devastating effect on these migratory fish, as they were unable to swim upstream of Bergerac. Fish ladders were constructed as soon as the problem was recognized, but they were not well designed and proved to be virtually useless. To add to this problem, in the 1930s and 40s the construction of hydro-electric dams high up on the Dordogne caused such fluctuations both in the flow and temperature of the water that the stocks of all kinds of river fish, not just migratory species, dropped dramatically.

The future looks considerably brighter, however, thanks to the energy and enthusiasm of conservationists such as Guy Pustelnik, founder of the aquarium museum in Sarlat. He

A wintery scene near Domme, where the Dordogne meanders through its wide plain.

helped to pioneer the installation of highly efficient fish ladders and even fish lifts, and to instigate a programme for restocking the river with Atlantic salmon. In 1993 more than a hundred salmon made their way up the Dordogne, a mark of the success of the programme, which is still in its early stages. Inevitably, the fishing of salmon from rivers is banned to allow them to increase in number, but there is hope that in the near future, freshly caught Dordogne salmon will once more be on offer in local restaurants. Shad are also beginning to return to the Dordogne, thanks to the fish ladders, and for the first time in 150 years, they are being landed fairly frequently even above Bergerac.

TOWARDS THE SEA

Between Bergerac and the sea, some 200 people still earn their living from fishing, catching mainly migratory fish such as lamprey, shad and eel, all of which provide reasonably lucrative returns. Eel is caught both in its adult state, and as elvers – *pibales* or *civelles* – which fetch enormous sums of money. With prices higher than 500F per kilogram, it is hardly surprising that their arrival causes enormous excitement, and all-night winter fishing expeditions are not uncommon.

Lampreys are a particular speciality of the region, and Claude Durand, a professional fisherman, does a roaring trade in them at Libourne market on Sundays. Carnivorous, leech-like creatures, with only a huge sucker for a mouth and no head as such, they are sold from mid-March until mid-May, alive and wriggling. (Another way to get a close view of a live lamprey is to visit the excellent Musée-Aquarium in Sarlat, where all of these river fish can be seen swimming around in tanks. The sight of the lampreys' suckers stuck firmly on to the glass wall of the tank is an image not easily forgotten.)

The classic dish, found throughout the region, is *lamproies à la bordelaise*, a rich stew cooked with red Bordeaux wine and leeks, but only the most intrepid of cooks would embark on this recipe. First, the lampreys must be stunned (although they can be killed more easily by immersing them quickly in boiling water), then each one must be nailed up by its tail while its head is slit in order to catch the blood, an essential ingredient in the dish. Several hours later, they must be skinned, gutted and cut up. After that, it is plain sailing: all that is needed is to soften an onion in melted fat, and make a roux with a little flour. Add a bottle of good red wine, together with the leeks, cut into rounds and browned lightly in walnut oil, and then simmer the whole lot for two hours. Finally, add the lampreys, either raw or pre-cooked in oil for a few minutes, and simmer for another 45 minutes. The result is a rich stew, which is often seen on restaurant menus in springtime.

Later in the season, in May, Claude Durand and many other fishermen turn their attention to catching shad, a delicious but rather bony fish which is a cousin of the herring. In the Bordelais, it is often grilled over *sarments* (vine cuttings) and served with a light shallot vinaigrette with chopped fresh herbs (see page 141). Sorrel is another favourite accompaniment, as its natural acidity balances the oiliness of the fish, and it is thought that it can dissolve the smallest fish bones.

VERJUICE

In the days before the arrival of cheap lemons, cooks often used the unfermented juice of sour grapes, or verjus, *to add piquancy to sauces for fish, chicken or rabbit. For centuries, the French cultivated special grape varieties to make verjuice, but nowadays it generally comes from unripe grapes harvested from vines before the autumn* vendange. *These grapes are gathered and crushed, then the sour juice is filtered before being bottled. For long a traditional ingredient in* périgourdin *cooking, verjuice also features in English medieval cookery books, made with the juice of crab apples. Verjuice is less harsh than lemon juice, and its subtle and slightly sweet acidity is ideal for accentuating delicate flavours. Nowadays, it is pasteurized so that it keeps well.*

Mamie Josette Landat, of the Domaine de Siorac, near Eymet, where verjuice is made, recalls her grandmother coming in from the vineyards with an apronful of green grapes which she would simply crush and use the same day, and laments the complications of making a modern version, which must keep, travel and look good. But travel it does, thanks to Bernard Lafon (see page 125) who has perfected the technique of bottling verjuice, and now sells it internationally.

TOP Poppies grow between rows of vines in the region of Monbazillac, making a colourful show.
ABOVE RIGHT Harvesting grapes by hand near Pomport, south-west of Bergerac.
ABOVE An invitation to buy regional produce.

WINE COUNTRY

In this region, the grape varieties are principally the same as those of the Bordelais: Cabernet Sauvignon, Cabernet Franc and Merlot for red; Sauvignon Blanc, Sémillon and Muscadelle for white, both sweet and dry. Although even at their best, Bergerac wines can never compete with the finest growths of neighbouring Saint-Emilion, Sauternes or the Médoc, the Bergeraçois possesses many of the vinous characteristics of Bordeaux in diminished scale, and its wines can be rich and powerful.

In recent years the area has aroused considerable interest, not just from French winemakers, but from Englishmen such as Henry Ryman, who bought Château de la Jaubertie in 1973. With the experimental approach of a newcomer, he has transformed the production into a range of exciting, full-flavoured wines and planted grape varieties such as Chenin Blanc and Chardonnay that are not typically grown here.

One of the most celebrated sweet wines of France, Monbazillac is the most famous of the Bergerac wines, with a history dating back to the fourteenth century. With its four round towers and stone mullioned windows, the Château de Monbazillac is also one of the prettiest in the region. It is owned by the Cave Coopérative, which opens it to the public, even in winter, and the old stables have been converted into a restaurant. Around the chateau, the vineyards face north, sloping gently towards the Dordogne river; thus they catch the misty

CHATEAU BELINGARD

*Château Belingard is the property of the
aristocratic Bosredon family, and has been
so, they are proud to recount, for the past 200
years. But the duration of their ownerships
seems like the blink of an eye compared with the
antiquity of the site itself. The name
Belingard comes from a Celtic word meaning
'garden of the gods', and according to
Laurent de Bosredon, the site contains an altar
stone that was used for druidic sacrificial
rites some 3,000 years ago. The Bosredons own
three other estates: Château Boudigand,
Château Chayne and the Abbaye Saint-Mayme,
and produce wines under the Bergerac, Côtes
de Bergerac and Monbazillac appellations. Their
Bergerac Sec is made with a high proportion
of Sauvignon grapes, and has a rich, perfumed
flavour that partners fish particularly well;
while the white Côtes de Bergerac has a small
amount of residual sugar, and is made
exclusively from the Sémillon grape.*

autumn dampness that encourages the growth of the microscopic fungus called botrytis or 'noble rot'. This causes the sought-after shrivelling of ripe grapes, so that their juice becomes more concentrated and the resulting wines richer and more luscious. Sémillon, Sauvignon Blanc and Muscadelle grapes are left on the vines as late as possible, sometimes until the end of November, in order to gain maximum sweetness and aroma, before they are harvested in stages. To reach its honeyed perfection, Monbazillac must be allowed to age and turn a rich amber colour. Much appreciated as an accompaniment to foie gras to begin a meal, or as a dessert wine to end it, such a lusciously sweet wine also complements salty cheese.

North of the Dordogne is the appellation of Pécharmant, producing full-bodied, rounded red wines on south-facing slopes of clay and limestone. A wine that needs ageing for five to seven years, Pécharmant is generally considered to be the best red wine of the Bergerac region. It is more substantial than red Bergerac, with a subtle and elegant nose, and partners the rich flavours of game and red meat very well. The vineyards of Pécharmant are scattered over four parishes: Bergerac, Creysse, Lembras and Saint-Sauveur, and locating a particular property can be difficult. Many consist of no more than one or two hectares, although one of the best, Château de Tiregand, is relatively large, with 35 hectares. Owned by François-Xavier de Saint-Exupéry, a cousin of the author of *Le Petit Prince*, the property has a lovely *chai de vieillissement* (wine store), dating from 1668, where the wines are aged in wooden barrels for between 12 and 18 months.

*ABOVE LEFT Vineyards in the region of Monbazillac,
where autumn mists rising from the river
encourage the growth of 'noble rot'.*

L'HOTEL DU PONT

GROLEJAC, TEL 53 28 15 94

There are no frills at the Hôtel du Pont – just paper tablecloths and plain bentwood chairs, with fishing nets for decoration in the dining-room. In front, the bar hums with life: there are lorry drivers and workmen, tourists and families with children. Locals often stop by for a quick drink after work or after picking mushrooms in the nearby woods.

People come to the restaurant for the freshwater fish. Bruno Jardel is the kind of chef who likes to keep things simple, and to keep prices down by offering the day's catch, whatever that happens to be. From June until October, there are eel, pike, carp and sandre *(pike-perch), and white fish such as bleak, perch, bream and barbel. Barbel and bream are too bony for most people's tastes nowadays, so they are made into* soupe de poissons, *which is served with croutons,* rouille *(a hot, chilli-spiced mayonnaise) and grated cheese.*

FRITURE DE LA DORDOGNE

Deep-Fried Small Fish with Garlic

Bruno Jardel uses bleak (ablettes) that he has netted himself for his friture *– a simple, rustic dish of crisply fried fish with a sprinkling of sliced garlic. The fish are roughly 10cm/4in long, about the size of sprats, which could also be cooked in this way. They are cleaned and gutted, but never washed after gutting as this could make them steam rather than cooking to a crisp finish. (Illustrated left)*

12–15 bleak per person
1 garlic clove per person
coarse sea salt and freshly ground black
pepper
oil, for frying

Heat the oil in a frying pan large enough to hold one serving of fish in a single layer. When the oil is smoking hot, arrange the fish side by side in the pan, and lower the heat. Cook for about 5 minutes, shaking the pan from time to time to prevent the fish from sticking. Turn

them over in one piece like a pancake, easing them on to a plate to do so. Strew with finely sliced garlic and salt and pepper and cook for another 5 minutes or until the underside is nicely browned. Serve immediately, with a glass of chilled white wine.

FILET DE SANDRE AU BEURRE BLANC

Fillet of Zander with Butter Sauce

The zander or pike-perch is a relative of the pike, and its flesh is equally sweet and fine-textured. Bruno Jardel fillets the fish, then poaches the fillets and serves them with a lemon-butter sauce. (Illustrated above)

SERVES 4
4 fillets of zander

FOR THE COURT-BOUILLON
2l/3½pt water
1 small onion
bouquet garni
12 peppercorns
2tsp salt
juice of 1 lemon

FOR THE SAUCE
juice of 1 lemon
225g/8oz cold butter, cut into small cubes
fresh parsley, chives and chervil, finely chopped

Bring the court-bouillon mixture to the boil, and simmer for 30 minutes so that the flavours amalgamate. Fold each fish fillet over length-wise, and place in the court-bouillon. Lower the heat, cover the pan, and simmer very gently, so that the liquid just shudders, for 30 minutes.

While the fish is cooking, prepare the sauce. Boil the lemon juice in a small saucepan until it reduces almost to nothing. Remove from heat and add the butter, a few cubes at a time, whisking vigorously to incorporate it into the sauce. Bring the sauce just back to the boil, whisking constantly, then take off the heat again. Add the herbs, and check seasoning.

When the fish is cooked, lift the fillets out of liquid with a slotted spoon, and serve with the sauce poured over.

BEIGNETS DE MORUE

Salt Cod Fritters

Sometimes called crépeaux, *these small, crisp savoury fritters are good to eat with apéritifs, or with salad as a starter or light lunch dish. La morue (dried and salted cod) can be bought on market stalls, stiff as a board and looking most unappetizing. It needs thorough soaking to get rid of the salt and pungent smell, but has the advantage that before soaking it will keep, in a cool and airy place, for many weeks. For this reason, salt cod was the staple Friday meal for Catholics who did not have any easy access to fresh sea-fish.*

MAKES 20–25 FRITTERS
350g/12oz salt cod, cut in large chunks
170g/6oz floury potatoes
3 eggs
140g/5oz flour
250ml/8fl oz milk
2tsp oil, for batter
oil, for frying

Soak the salt cod in water for 48 hours, changing the water every 12 hours, then drain it. Bring a large pan of water to the boil (do not salt the water) and take off the heat. Place the pieces of cod in the water, put back on the heat, cover and bring to the boil again. Poach gently for 15 minutes. Drain, and remove the skin and bones from the fish, flaking the flesh as you work. Peel the potatoes, and boil in salted water. Drain thoroughly, and mash. Mix the mashed potato with the cooked salt cod, and blend in one of the egg yolks (you can do this in a food processor). Reserve the white in a separate bowl until ready to finish cooking.

Separate the other 2 eggs, and mix the yolks with the flour, milk and batter oil in a food processor, turning it on just for a second or two, until the ingredients are blended. Season lightly with salt, and set aside for an hour before using.

When ready to cook, whisk the single egg white until stiff, and incorporate into the salt cod mixture as lightly as possible, so that it does not collapse.

Whisk the other 2 egg whites together until stiff, and incorporate gently into the batter mixture. Heat the oil for frying in a frying-pan or deep-fat fryer.

Using a teaspoon, form balls of salt cod mixture about the size of a walnut, and dip each into the batter. When the oil is hot, drop in the balls and fry until golden brown and crisp, turning over if necessary from time to time. Drain on paper towels, and serve immediately.

ECREVISSES DE VERGT

Crayfish with Tomato Sauce

Chalky streams are the natural habitat of fresh-water crayfish, curious creatures that resemble miniature lobsters. La Mazille, in La Bonne Cuisine du Périgord, describes how easy it was to catch crayfish by donning a pair of espadrilles and paddling around in shallow streams, lifting every stone to reveal, with any luck, one or two écrevisses, which could be picked up and dropped into a bucket.

Today, crayfish are farmed, and they can sometimes be bought frozen from fishmongers. Frozen crayfish have the advantage of being ready cleaned; otherwise recipes such as this one that call for raw crayfish mean that the intestines have to be removed from the live crayfish, a difficult and unpleasant task. Although there is not much meat to be found on a crayfish, the pleasure in eating them comes mainly from the sauce, and sucking the juices from their shells. (Illustrated opposite)

SERVES 4 AS A MAIN COURSE OR 8 AS A STARTER
2tbsp walnut or olive oil
4 dozen crayfish, cleaned
3 glasses white wine
1 liqueur glass cognac
4 tomatoes, peeled, deseeded and chopped

FOR THE SAUCE
1tbsp oil
115g/4oz each chopped carrot, onion, celery
2 garlic cloves
2 or 3 shallots
thyme
bay leaf
salt and freshly ground black pepper

If the crayfish are frozen, first allow them to defrost thoroughly. In a saucepan, heat the walnut or olive oil, and throw in the crayfish, which will quickly turn red. Moisten with the white wine, pour in the cognac, then set it alight. Extinguish the flames by adding the chopped tomatoes, cover and cook for 5 minutes Then take off the heat, remove the crayfish with a slotted spoon and set aside. Reserve the cooking bouillon.

In another pan, heat the oil for the sauce, add the other ingredients, cover, and cook for 30 minutes over gentle heat. Add the bouillon from the crayfish, and cook for another 10 minutes. Strain through a fine sieve, pushing some of the vegetables through the sieve with a ladle or wooden spoon, to thicken the sauce lightly. Check the seasoning.

Either serve the crayfish in their shells for guests to deal with themselves, or peel and reheat them gently in the sauce before serving with good crusty bread to mop up the juices.

SALADE AUX TOPINAMBOURS

Jerusalem Artichoke Salad

Although the pleasant, sweetish flavour of these knobbly roots is not totally unlike that of globe artichokes, Jerusalem artichokes are misleadingly named. They are not artichokes in fact, nor do they come from Jerusalem, the word being a corruption of the French girasol, *as the tall plant is related to the sunflower. They were first imported to France from North America at the beginning of the 17th century. With an earthier flavour than globe artichokes, these roots are particularly good in soups and, more surprisingly, in salads such as this one.*

This salad can be served as part of a mixed hors d'oeuvre, especially with charcuterie, as its sweetness contrasts well with salty saucisson, jambon de pays *or a relatively new regional speciality,* magret séché – *duck breast ham.*

SERVES 4–6
450g/1lb Jerusalem artichokes
1tsp Dijon mustard
1tbsp chopped capers or pickled nasturtium seeds (see page 59)
2tbsp chopped pickled gherkins
2tbsp chopped parsley
175ml/6fl oz mayonnaise, made with 1 egg yolk, 1tbsp white wine vinegar and 150ml/5fl oz oil

Peel the artichokes in water containing a little lemon juice or vinegar, to prevent them from going brown. Simmer in salted water until soft. While they are cooking, mix all of the other ingredients with the mayonnaise. When the artichokes are cooked, drain well, and while still warm, slice them and coat with the sauce. Cover and refrigerate until ready to serve.

PUREE D'OSEILLE

Sorrel Purée

The sharp, lemony flavour of sorrel makes a good contrast with rich, fatty meat dishes, such as confit *of duck or goose.*

450g/1lb sorrel
1tbsp goose fat or butter
100ml/3½fl oz chicken stock
chopped parsley or chervil
salt and freshly ground black pepper

Clean the sorrel, and remove stalks. Blanch for 1 minute in boiling water, drain thoroughly and chop. Melt the fat in a saucepan, and add sorrel and stock. Stir around, and simmer over gentle heat for about 30 minutes. During this time, it will reduce to a purée, and change from bright green to a dull khaki. Stir in the chopped parsley or chervil, season to taste and serve.

CAROTTES NOUVELLES AUX RAISINS

Young Carrots with Pickled Grapes

Pickled prunes, cherries and pears are excellent accompaniments to roast or grilled meat, and in this recipe, pickled grapes are cooked with carrots to make a sweet-and-sour vegetable dish. (Illustrated on page 117)

SERVES 4
1tbsp of sugar
1tsp honey
100ml/3½fl oz white wine vinegar
115g/4oz of small, seedless green grapes, washed and with stalks removed
sprig of tarragon

550g/1¼lb young carrots
1tbsp butter
300g/10½oz baby onions, peeled but whole
100ml/3½fl oz dry white wine
1tbsp crème fraîche
salt and freshly ground black pepper

To make the pickled grapes, first dissolve the sugar and honey in the vinegar, and bring to the boil. Put the grapes into a clean glass jar, push the tarragon down among them, and pour the boiling vinegar over. Seal with an airtight lid, and store in a cool, dark place for two weeks or more to allow the flavour to develop.

Peel or scrub the carrots. Melt the butter in a heavy saucepan or cast-iron casserole, and brown the whole onions. Add the carrots, season with salt and pepper, then pour in the liquid from the jar of grapes, mixed with the white wine. Cover tightly and cook slowly for 45 minutes.

When the carrots are cooked, add the grapes and crème fraîche, and simmer for a few minutes more, with the pan uncovered, until almost no liquid remains.

BROCHET DE L'ISLE A LA SAUCE VERTE

Poached Pike with Green Herb Sauce

In France, pike is thought to be one of the finest of fish, while in Britain it is not highly regarded at all, and fishermen rarely eat their catch, believing it to be too bony and muddy-flavoured. In fact, pike caught from clean, flowing water should not taste muddy at all, and by poaching it whole in a court-bouillon, the fish can then be skinned and the fillets lifted off with ease. (Illustrated opposite)

SERVES 6
1 pike weighing about 2.3kg/5lb
6 juniper berries, crushed

FOR THE COURT-BOUILLON
500ml/16fl oz white wine
1 liqueur glass eau-de-vie
10 whole black peppercorns
5 juniper berries
sprig of fennel
bouquet garni
3 shallots
1 carrot, sliced lengthwise
1 onion, sliced across

FOR THE SAUCE
8tbsp olive oil
2tbsp white wine vinegar or verjuice
2 shallots, finely chopped
2tbsp finely chopped parsley
1tbsp finely chopped fresh tarragon
1tbsp finely chopped chervil
1tbsp capers or pickled nasturtium seeds

To scale the fish, plunge it in boiling water, leave for a few seconds, then take it out and drain. Remove the scales with a sharp knife. Plunge into cold water to firm the flesh, then rub with coarse salt and crushed juniper berries, and leave in a cool place for an hour.

Wash the fish in cold water, then place in a fish kettle with the ingredients for the court-bouillon, cover and bring to the boil. As soon as it boils, turn down the heat and continue to cook very gently, so that the liquid trembles slightly but doesn't boil, for half an hour.

To make the sauce, whisk oil and vinegar together to make an emulsion, add other ingredients, and season with salt and pepper.

When the fish is cooked, carefully lift it out of the liquid, remove the skin, take the fish off the bone, and serve the fillets with the sauce.

Maurice Jardel (seated) and his son Bruno, pulling in the fishing nets from a quiet backwater, un bras mort, of the Dordogne river. Cutting steeply into the limestone cliffs on the other side, the backwater almost forms an ox-bow lake, where the water is less turbulent than the main part of the river. It is a good place to catch pike, zander, bream, barbel and bleak, which come to feed in the calm water, and to shelter from the strong current of the river.

BROCHET FARCI CAYRE

Stuffed Pike with Lemon Sauce

Jean-Noël Cayre's hotel-restaurant is right on the bank of the Dordogne, and many of his specialities come from the river. His father, Jean-Louis, is the fisherman of the family, and his son, Eric, is the chef.

Jean-Noël Cayre likes to stuff pike with beurre à l'escargot, *the classic stuffing for snails – garlic butter flavoured with parsley. He then serves the fish with a lemon sauce made from the cooking juices.*

SERVES 8
85g/3oz butter
2 garlic cloves, finely chopped
55g/2oz streaky bacon, finely diced
3tbsp chopped parsley
1 pike, weighing no more than 2kg/4½lb, gutted and cleaned
6 shallots, chopped
250ml/8fl oz white wine
30g/1oz flour
squeeze of lemon juice
1tbsp chopped chervil
salt and freshly ground black pepper

Preheat the oven to 180°C/350°F/gas mark 4. Mash 55g/2oz of the butter with the garlic, bacon and parsley, and season with salt and pepper. Use this mixture to stuff the fish.

Butter a baking tin or flame-proof dish, and put in the chopped shallots. Place the pike on top, sprinkle with some of the wine, cover with foil, and bake in the oven for 45–50 minutes, until cooked through.

Take the fish out of the dish, and carefully remove the skin. Lift the fillets from the bone, and put them to one side, keeping them warm while you make the sauce.

Pour the remaining wine into the cooking juices to deglaze, and strain the liquid into a saucepan. Bring to the boil, simmer for 10 minutes. Work the flour into the remaining butter, and then use this *beurre manié* to thicken the sauce, by dropping pieces of the paste into it and whisking as you do so. Check seasoning, add a squeeze of lemon if necessary to sharpen the sauce, stir in the chopped chervil, and serve with the pike fillets.

FILET DE TRUITE AUX NOIX

Trout Fillets with Walnut Sauce

The hotel-restaurant Saint-Albert, in Sarlat, is a bastion of tradition, where you can get tourain blanchi, confit de canard, pommes sarladaises, gâteau aux noix *and other local favourites. This is one of their ways of serving trout, with a deliciously creamy walnut sauce; it is not strictly a regional dish, but very good all the same.*

SERVES 4
4 trout, filleted
250ml/8fl oz fish stock
4 shallots, finely chopped
splash of *vin de noix* (walnut aperitif) or semi-sweet white wine
250ml/8fl oz crème fraîche
55g/2oz walnuts, finely chopped

Poach the fish fillets in the stock, then take out of the liquid and keep warm. Add the shallots and *vin de noix* to the stock. Bring to the boil, and reduce for 5 minutes. Add the crème fraîche and chopped walnuts, season and allow to bubble for another 5 minutes or so, until the sauce will coat the back of the spoon. Skin the fish, pour the sauce over, and serve.

MATELOTE D'ANGUILLE AU VIN DE CAHORS

Eel Stewed in Red Wine

Jean-Noël Cayre, of the hotel-restaurant bearing his name at Rouffilhac, serves eel caught by his father, Jean-Louis. He describes his way of cooking it as 'just like coq au vin', and so it is – in a rich sauce of red wine, mushrooms, onions and tiny lardons of bacon.

SERVES 6
3tbsp grapeseed or sunflower seed oil
1kg/2¼lb eel, gutted, skinned and cut into
10cm/4in lengths
2 onions, thinly sliced
1 carrot, sliced
sprig of thyme
bay leaf
bouquet garni
1 bottle of Cahors wine
2 garlic cloves, finely chopped
12 shallots, peeled
1tsp sugar
225g/8oz button mushrooms
115g/4oz bacon, diced
***beurre manié*, made with 1½tbsp flour and**
2tbsp butter

Heat a tablespoon of oil in a large lidded pan, and brown the eel for about 10 minutes, turning over to cook on all sides. With a slotted spoon, take out the eel, and set aside while you cook the vegetables. Put the sliced onion, carrot, thyme, bay leaf and bouquet garni into the pan, stir around over gentle heat for 15 minutes, then pour in the red wine. Bring to the boil, cover, and simmer for 30 minutes, then put the pieces of eel, together with the garlic, into the pan, season with salt and pepper, and stew gently for a further 30 minutes.

Meanwhile, heat a tablespoon of oil in a small pan, and brown the shallots lightly over a gentle heat. Dust them with sugar, cook briefly taking care not to let them burn, then barely cover the shallots with water, and simmer gently without a lid for 20 minutes. Sauté the mushrooms and bacon separately in oil, and drain before serving.

When the eel is cooked, take it out of its cooking liquid and put it on one side, keeping it warm while you finish the sauce. Gently work the butter and flour together to make a *beurre manié*, and drop small pieces of this paste, one by one, into the sauce to thicken it, stirring as you do so. Bring the sauce to the boil, stirring constantly, and simmer briefly over gentle heat.

Place the cooked shallots, mushrooms and bacon on a serving dish with the eel, and pour the sauce over. Serve immediately.

GATEAU DE MORUE

Salt Cod Purée with Potatoes and Walnut Oil

Since medieval times, dried and salted cod has formed an important part of people's diet in inland France, where in the past, fresh fish was not available. The dried fish was brought from the North Atlantic, then transported into the French mainland on river barges up the Dordogne, and eventually to the Auvergne and Rouergue, where estofinado, a similiar dish to the one described here, became a speciality.

Even now, the board-like pieces of morue séchée (dried cod) are a familiar sight on market stalls, along with other preserved foods such as dried beans and lentils, olives and capers, and they are still popular, despite their high price and the competition from fresh fish.

SERVES 4
550g/1¼lb salt cod
5tbsp walnut oil
5tbsp grapeseed oil
3 garlic cloves, finely chopped
550g/1¼lb floury potatoes, peeled and
roughly chopped
3 eggs, separated
2tbsp chopped fresh parsley

TO SERVE
2 hard-boiled eggs, quartered
triangles of fried bread

Soak the salt cod for 24 hours, changing the water at least 3 times, then drain and put in a pan with fresh water. Bring very slowly to the boil, then take off the heat, and leave, covered, for 20 minutes. Remove the cod with a slotted spoon, retaining the cooking water, and flake, discarding skin and bones. Add the oil and chopped garlic, and work together until smooth, either by hand or in a food processor. Keep warm.

Preheat the oven to 190°C/375°F/gas mark 5.

Boil the chopped potatoes in the cooking water from the fish. When they are cooked, mash them to a purée, and then beat in the egg yolks. Whisk the egg whites briskly in a separate bowl until stiff.

Mix the cod and potatoes together thoroughly, add the chopped parsley, check the seasoning, and adjust it if necessary. Then carefully fold in the egg whites.

Pour the mixture into a greased baking dish, drizzle with a little more walnut oil, and cook for about 40–45 minutes. During baking the 'gâteau' will rise and become golden brown in colour.

Serve very hot, garnished with quarters of hard-boiled egg and triangles of fried bread, and accompanied by a green salad.

POULET AU VERJUS

Chicken with Verjuice

Verjuice, made from the juice of unripe grapes, can be bought in France in bottles or in jars which also contain whole green grapes. It is often used to deglaze the pan juices after sautéing chicken or trout; here, the chicken is actually cooked in the verjuice, which gives a pleasant sour-sweetness to the sauce. Bramley apple juice sharpened with a squeeze of lemon can substitute for verjuice.

SERVES 6
6 chicken legs, with thigh attached
1tbsp goose fat
12 small onions
1 x 170g/6oz jar of verjuice with green grapes *or* 18 seedless grapes and 175ml/6fl oz verjuice
300ml/10fl oz chicken stock, preferably home-made
3 garlic cloves, finely chopped
salt and freshly ground black pepper
2tbsp chopped parsley, for garnish

Rub salt and pepper into the skin of the chicken. Melt the goose fat in a large casserole or sauté pan with a lid, and add the chicken portions, skin side down, and the small onions, peeled but whole. Cook briefly over fairly high heat, then turn and cook until both sides are nicely browned. Remove the chicken from the pan, spoon off excess fat, then add the verjuice and stock, scraping the brown bits from the bottom of the pan. Replace the chicken, cover the pan, and simmer for 30 minutes.

Add grapes to the sauce, sprinkle with chopped garlic, and cover the pan again. Leave over the gentlest heat for 5 minutes, then sprinkle with chopped parsley, and serve.

CAILLES DE VIGNE

Quail with Grapes

Quail was once a rare treat, savoured only when a hunter had been lucky. Now they are bred specially for the table, and are more tender and juicy than wild ones. In wine-growing areas, they are wrapped in vine leaves to preserve their moisture while cooking, and served with green grapes. When grapes are not available, raisins soaked in a mixture of water and eau-de-vie may be used instead.

SERVES 4
8 quail
8 vine leaves, stems removed
8 slices streaky bacon
1tbsp duck fat
175ml/6fl oz semi-sweet white wine
450g/1lb small white grapes
salt and freshly ground black pepper

Preheat the oven to 220°C/425°F/gas mark 7. Wrap the breast of each quail first in a vine leaf, then tie on a slice of bacon. In a shallow oven-proof dish, heat the duck fat, and put the quail into the hot fat. Pour over half of the wine, and place half of the grapes around the birds. Place in the oven and cook for 15 minutes. Remove bacon and vine leaves, and return to the oven for a few minutes, so that the breasts brown.

Simmer the remaining grapes in the rest of the wine until soft, then remove them.

Transfer the quail and grapes to a serving dish when they are cooked, and keep warm. Pour off the excess fat from the cooking juices, then add them to the wine in which the grapes were cooked, and reduce by one-third.

Check the seasoning, and serve the sauce with the quail and grapes.

GIGOT PERIGOURDIN A LA COURONNE D'AIL

Leg of Lamb with a Crown of Garlic

In the past, in regions where wood was plentiful, food would have been cooked over a smouldering fire. A covered cast-iron pot with a concave lid (upon which could be heaped hot cinders) was used to create an enclosed cooking space, rather like a small oven. The fire would be kept low, not only for the sake of economy, but also so that the food would gently braise, until the meat was tender enough to fall off the bone. (Illustrated right)

SERVES 8
1 tbsp goose fat
1 leg of lamb, weighing about 2–2½kg/4–5lb, with the skin removed
50–60 garlic cloves
1 liqueur glass brandy or eau-de-vie
2 wine glasses Monbazillac wine
salt and freshly ground black pepper

Preheat the oven to 120°C/250°F/gas mark ½. Heat the goose fat in a cast-iron casserole large enough to take the leg of lamb, and brown the meat on all sides in the fat. Pack the peeled garlic cloves around the meat, then pour the brandy over it, and set it alight. When the flames have died down, add the sweet white wine, and season with salt and pepper.

Cover tightly with a lid, and put the casserole in a low oven for about 4 hours.

Serve the lamb surrounded by its crown of garlic, with the pan juices and vegetables.

OPPOSITE Leg of Lamb with a Crown of Garlic, served with Young Carrots with Pickled Grapes (page 112) and a purée of broad beans.

GATEAU RENVERSE

Apple and Prune Upside-down Cake

Apples and prunes are particularly good together, the tartness of the apples balanced by the sweet richness of fat Agen prunes. Bathed in buttery juices, they combine to form a beautiful pattern of black and gold on the top of this cake. (Illustrated left)

SERVES 6
300g/10oz Agen prunes
125g/4½oz butter
125g/4½oz sugar
2 large or 3 small eating apples, such as
Cox's
1 egg
3tbsp milk
150g/5oz self-raising flour
cold black tea, for soaking prunes

Soak prunes for 2 hours in cold tea, then drain and remove stones.

Preheat the oven to 200°C/400°F/gas mark 6. Cream 55g/2oz each of the butter and sugar together, until smooth and of even consistency. This can be done in a food processor. Spread the mixture over the base and sides of a cake tin measuring 24cm/9½in. The tin should not have a removable base, or the juices will tend to leak out during cooking.

Peel, core and slice the apples, and arrange, with the prunes, over the butter-sugar mixture until all are used up.

Mix the remaining butter with the rest of the sugar, and add the egg and milk, beating well, then blend in the flour to make a fairly thick cake mixture.

Spread the mixture evenly over the apples and prunes, and bake for about 35 minutes, or until the cake tests cooked with a skewer, which should emerge clean once plunged into the cake. Leave for a few minutes to cool slightly, then turn out the cake on to a serving plate, having first loosened the sides with a knife. Serve warm, with dollops of cold crème fraîche.

SOUPE DE FRAISES AU VIN DE GLANES

Strawberry Soup with Glanes Red Wine

At the Hôtel Fournié in Beaulieu-sur-Dordogne, two local specialities are combined in this refreshing summertime dessert.

Sweet, juicy Gariguette strawberries flourish on the sandy soils that border the river – here they are macerated in the little-known Vin de Pays des Coteaux de Glanes, made from Gamay and Merlot grapes that grow on the hills above St Céré. (Illustrated right)

SERVES 6
1 bottle vin de Glanes, or similar
red wine
vanilla pod
½ cinnamon stick
150g/5½oz sugar
1 kg/2¼lb strawberries, hulled

In a saucepan over a gentle heat, slowly bring the wine, vanilla, cinnamon and sugar to the boil, taking care to dissolve the sugar before the liquid boils. When boiling, burn off the alcohol by holding a lighted match close to the hot wine. Leave to cool. When the wine is lukewarm, pour it over the fruit, and leave to macerate in a cool place overnight.

Serve the soup on its own, or with fresh whipped cream.

ABOVE Château Pichon Longueville, its elegant corner turrets creating the impression of a fairytale castle, is one of the great wine properties of the Médoc. It is owned by AXA, one of France's largest insurance companies. Classified in 1855 as second growth, on a par with Mouton-Rothschild, the wines are classic Pauillacs, often very tough and tannic at first, acquiring a rich, velvety texture with maturity.
RIGHT Wooden oyster cabanes in Gujan-Mestras, on the shores of the Bay of Arcachon.
FAR RIGHT Obsolete posters remain intact for years.

THE BORDELAIS

In the most important, most complicated and most prestigious wine region in the world, food inevitably tends to play second fiddle. *La cuisine bordelaise* has never been the subject of much interest in the eyes of the world, and is often overlooked completely, or regarded merely as a necessary but rather tiresome accompaniment to wine. In reality, Bordeaux's best restaurants are as elegant as its architecture, its cooking as refined as that of any other French city, and the variety and quality of local ingredients of the highest order. Nonetheless, chefs are only too aware that most of their customers are there for the wine, and compose their menus accordingly, to complement it. Most of the traditional Bordelais dishes revolve around simple treatments of the best ingredients, for the same reason.

CITY LIFE

With its cosmopolitan outlook and feeling of prosperity, Bordeaux derives its wealth not only from wine, but also from its position as the premier port of south-west France. The elegant white-stone façades of its riverside buildings, its squares and courtyards, its neo-classical theatre and sweeping avenues tell us that the eighteenth century was the golden age for Bordeaux. The wine trade was flourishing; colonies in the West Indies were supplying sugar, coffee and cocoa, which were consumed in great quantities in the city's fashionable cafés; amber, ebony and ivory came also from the colonies, and fat profits were made from the slave trade. From inland came grain and timber, building stone and all manner of foods: ceps and truffles, wild game and poultry, fruit and vegetables. The bay of Arcachon provided a safe harbour for deep-sea fishing boats, and shelter for the raising of oysters. It was a period of great prosperity, and the population of the city doubled between 1715 and 1790.

Today, the interests of the city are spread between the deliberate policy of industrialization, and its cultural and artistic pursuits. Bordeaux has several important museums and art galleries, including the recently opened Cité Mondiale du Vin et des Spiritueux exhibition centre. The city hosts the annual 'Mai Musical' festival and the biennial Vinexpo, the most important exhibition of wine in the world. It is officially reserved for professionals, but any serious wine-lover with a friend in the trade should beg for a ticket.

CONFIT DE
Poule
55 Foo Pièce
150 Foo les 3

COQ AU VIN
85 Foo Pièce
150 Foo les 2

*Scenes from Bordeaux: the city's classical
waterfront façades (top) were a
source of delight for 18th-century engravers.
Here, along the banks of the Garonne,
wine shippers have long had their
headquarters, but today, as well as being
a centre of the wine trade, the city
enjoys a reputation for its lively bistrots,
its sophisticated food markets
and pavement cafés.*

A good deal of wine-tasting also goes on in the city's hundreds of lively wine bars and bistrots, where a chalked menu of the day includes such wine-friendly dishes as *huîtres et saucisses grillées* – small, spicy sausages called *lou kencous*, which are eaten with a plate of oysters and washed down with a glass of chilled white Graves or Entre-Deux-Mers, *coeur de veau braisé au vin rouge, tête de veau ravigote, lamproies à la bordelaise* or *côtes de mouton grillées*. Oyster bars abound in the city centre, often serving steaming dishes of *moules marinières* or *huîtres chaudes* (see page 139), for those who don't like live oysters.

THE MARKETS AND SHOPS OF BORDEAUX

For anyone with an interest in gastronomy, Bordeaux is one of the most exciting cities in France to visit. The food markets range from the brash, noisy Marché des Capucins, which opens every day from midnight to midday in a gloomy space below a car park, but is noted for its excellent fresh seafood, to the organic Thursday market in the Place Saint-Pierre, where market cafés serve oysters and white wine for lunch; then there is the Saturday *marché fermier* around the church of Saint-Michel, and the elegant Galeries des Grands Hommes, a superb modern building containing a number of high-quality food shops.

Many of the streets in the city centre have been pedestrianized, which makes shopping a relaxing pastime. Highlights include *artisan-fromager* Jean d'Alos in rue Montesquieu, one of the finest cheese shops in France, where as many as 250 different kinds of cheese are displayed on traditional straw mats. Below the shop are ancient tunnels, the cellars of a former convent, where Jean d'Alos matures the cheeses, turning and brushing them as necessary until they reach perfection. Another superb cheese shop is Antonin, in rue Fondaudège, which has as many as 60 different *chèvres*. At Cadiot-Badie in the Allées de Tourny, a wonderfully old-fashioned chocolate shop with an 1826 façade, you can buy exquisite handmade chocolates: crunchy *praslines de Blaye* (almonds coated with sugary praline), *huîtres d'Arcachon* (chocolate oysters filled with praline or marzipan) and dozens of other tempting treats. There are five branches of Dastarac, the most celebrated of Bordeaux *boulangeries*, with its wonderful selection of breads and brioches, while at Pain Maître they specialize in organic sourdough bread. Another Bordeaux institution, founded over a hundred years ago, is the Charcuterie de Tours in rue Michel de Montaigne, which also operates as a *traiteur*, selling ready-cooked meals. If you want to sample a speciality of Bordeaux, the best *cannelés* (see page 145) are reputed to come from Bonnaud, and should be eaten within the day. Also not to be missed is the patisserie Darricau, with its frescoed first-floor *salon de thé*.

Not surprisingly, Bordeaux boasts a number of outstanding wine shops. L'Intendant, a Guggenheim museum of wine with a beautiful spiral cellar, five floors deep, beneath the tiny shop, has bottles from 50 to 15,000F, including all of the great vintages. Cousin & Compagnie is a relative newcomer to the wine scene, run by a group of bright young men who work with the *negoçiants* to get the lowest possible prices both for the great Bordelais wines, and for those of *petits châteaux*. As well as a wide range of local wines, they offer a few bottles from other parts of France which represent especially good value, and run regular tastings.

LILLET

Originally created by Lillet Frères at Podensac in 1872, the Bordeaux aperitif, Lillet, had its heyday before the Second World War when it became fashionable throughout France. Today, it is no longer widely known outside Bordeaux, although, curiously, it is apparently much sought after in Manhattan. Lillet is an aromatic aperitif à base de vin: a local Gironde wine is mixed with various fruit liqueurs, made by macerating fresh fruit in brandy for several months. The liquid is then filtered and matured in oak vats for six months. It is served chilled or on the rocks, sometimes with a twist of orange or lemon. Faced with declining sales, a decision was made to relaunch Lillet in 1986 and since then the drink has started to regain its old popularity. The new version is less fierce and cloying than the old, and has a smoother, more aromatic taste. Both red and white forms of the drink have a pleasant hint of bitterness with a slight scent of oranges and other fruits.

ABOVE A mixture of finely-chopped parsley and garlic, known variously as le hachis *or* le persillade, *is an integral ingredient often used to complement the flavour of south-western dishes.*
BELOW Hot, spicy sausages and cold, fresh oysters, washed down with a glass of chilled white wine such as Graves or Entre-Deux-Mers, is a speciality at restaurant Chez Philippe (see page 134).

LA CUISINE BORDELAISE

Links between the Bordelais countryside and the city at its heart have always been close, and remain so even today. With such a rich variety of ingredients, it is hardly surprising that cooks have tended to treat food in the most straightforward way possible, adding sauces and flavourings only to bring out the best in their raw materials.

The other notable feature of Bordelais cuisine is that food is usually quickly cooked, rather than slowly simmered as in Périgord; this may have stemmed from the shortage of freely available firewood in the past. Although timber was brought to Bordeaux on the river from the forests of Cantal and Auvergne, it was largely needed for construction purposes – barrel-making and for making vine stakes – so was too valuable to burn in any quantity. Instead of wasting precious fuel on long simmering, meat and fish were often grilled quickly instead, sometimes over a fire of broken barrels, as in *entrecôte à la bordelaise* (see page 142), sometimes over vine cuttings, as in *alose grillée* (see page 141).

According to the Bordeaux restaurateur Félix Desplanches (1835-1912), who wrote (under the pseudonym Alcide Bontou) the classic Bordeaux cookery book, *Traité de Cuisine Bourgeoise Bordelaise*, the best place to eat *entrecôte à la bordelaise* was among the wine barrels stored in the *chai*. There the cooper and cellar master could sometimes be found cooking their steaks over a fire made from old chestnut casks, which apparently gave the meat a superbly aromatic flavour. According to the food writer Curnonsky, vineyard rats were once grilled in this way, and known as steak *tonnelier* ('barrel-maker' steak).

The term *à la bordelaise* is the source of much confusion, and means a variety of things to different people. It can mean a dish containing shallots, for example, or garlic and parsley, sometimes with the addition of marrowbone, or a dish containing ceps or artichoke bottoms and potatoes. *Sauce bordelaise* is usually made with red wine, shallots and beef marrow, although the illustrious nineteenth-century Parisian chef Antonin Carême made his with Sauternes, garlic, tarragon and provençal olive oil – so it is far from being a fixed recipe.

Shallots are the only consistent link, and they play a prominent part in Bordelais cooking, as important as garlic in Périgord and Quercy. It is thought that they were brought to Aquitaine from Palestine by the British, and were found to thrive in the fertile, well-drained soils of the river valleys of the Gironde. They have a less acrid flavour than onions and are mild enough to eat raw, although they are usually lightly cooked. There are several varieties, with red, brown and yellow skins, but those with brown skins are the most common.

Meat that is to be cooked quickly needs to be very tender, and one of the great specialities of the Bordelais region is *l'agneau de Pauillac*, traditionally reared on the salt marshes of the Médoc, although now it also comes from pastures of the Graves and the Landes. Fed exclusively on milk, the lambs are raised in barns and slaughtered at the age of six to eight weeks. At this age, they weigh only about 12 kilograms and the meat is pale in colour and meltingly tender. The season for *l'agneau de Pauillac* is fairly short, and lasts only from January until Easter, so summer visitors are likely to miss it altogether. Roasted or grilled, sometimes with the new season's garlic, there is no better partner for a good claret than this uncomplicated food.

BERNARD LAFON

Bernard Lafon remembers his grandmother gathering wild mushrooms, nettles and sorrel in the woods near her house in Sadirac, and using them to make soup or an omelette on the open kitchen fire. Years later and tired of city life, he returned home to the family estate, where these childhood memories inspired him to set up a small business selling wild, old or rare varieties of vegetables and plants, such as nettles, samphire, sorrel and seaweed. The nettles grow in neighbouring fields and at harvest time are simply stripped from their stalks and sterilized in low-temperature spring water. Other vegetables and fruits – Chinese artichokes, cape gooseberries, griotte cherries, baby pears – are preserved in sour-sweet pickling vinegar, flavoured with tarragon, juniper berries, coriander, pepper and mustard. Lafon's mission is to fight against the blandness of today's food by bringing a touch of originality back to cooking; his latest venture has been to pioneer the reintroduction of verjuice in Périgord (see page 105) and to make mustard with verjuice according to a medieval recipe.

ABOVE Bordeaux's wealth of classical buildings are graceful and elegant, yet retain a pleasant informality. Many, such as this one, are topped by a mansard roof, and decorated with gargoyles. RIGHT Crispy and sweet on the outside, soft in the centre, les cannelés are one of Bordeaux's best-known specialities. They can be enjoyed at any time - with a cup of coffee or tea, or accompanied by a glass of sweet white wine. They can bought at most of the city's patisseries, or made at home, using the recipe on page 145.

The region around Bazas, south of the Garonne, is famous for its beef, *le boeuf gris de Bazas* (*gris* refers to the colour of its coat). It comes from an old breed of cattle that is castrated at about 11 or 12 months old, then let out to graze for three years. After two years of being fattened in the cattle-shed the beasts are slaughtered, by which time the marbled meat is tender and tasty and perfect for *entrecôte à la bordelaise*.

Every region in France has its own charcuterie, and in the Bordelais there are *les grattons de Lormont* – Boucherie Martin in Cadillac makes the best. Quite unlike the *grattons* of the Lyonnais, this is made from long-cooked chunks of succulent ham and shoulder of pork and is more like a terrine, served cold, cut into neat slices, and it is very good for picnics. It can also be bought at La Maison du Jambon in nearby Beguey, where the Pyrenean mountain ham is also highly recommended.

OYSTERS

In June the small fishing village of Gujon-Mestras,
on the shores of the Bay of Arcachon, bustles
with activity. Clay pantiles painted with
limewash are stacked in the sun waiting for the
time when the oysters will start to breed.
At exactly the right moment, the tiles are stacked
on trolleys and pushed down railtracks to
be placed in the sea. Once in the water, floating
microscopic oyster larvae attach themselves
to the limewashed surface, where they start to
grow. After eight or ten months, the tiles
are recovered and the tiny oysters, weighing only
about a gram, stripped off. These small oysters
are then taken out in cages to the parc à huîtres,
where they continue to grow for another
three or four years.
In l970, a parasitic attack wiped out the
entire oyster stock at Arcachon. Today, however,
the old Portuguese plates *have been replaced*
by gigas, *a fast-growing, hardier variety from the*
Pacific, and the oyster beds are among the
most productive in France.

TO THE SEA

In Bordeaux, oysters are rather taken for granted, and sold at prices that to the rest of the world seem very low, much to the chagrin of the cultivators in the Bay of Arcachon. Contrary to appearances, oysters demand much care and attention, and the *ostréiculteur* must have a vast fund of knowledge in order to succeed. Oysters have been raised in vast *parcs* in the bay for over a century, but today mussels, clams and cockles are also cultivated and experimental farming of migratory fish such as salmon and sturgeon is under way.

Until the middle of the eighteenth century it was believed that the supply of wild oysters in the Bay of Arcachon was inexhaustible, but by the 1750s demand was so great that oyster-gathering had to be forbidden. Despite these precautions, the depletion continued, and it was eventually realized that if the Bordelais were to continue to enjoy oysters, they would have to be cultivated. It was then that a scientist called Coste, the father of the oyster industry, conceived the idea of copying the techniques of oyster cultivation employed by the Italians, in order to produce cheap food for the French, and it was he who initiated the methods that are used today in Arcachon.

There are over 300 types of oyster in the world, but those found in south-west France are limited to the fine-flavoured *Ostrea edulis*, known as *plates* (meaning flat); *Crassotrea angulata*, the more robust, cheaper Portuguese oyster, *l'huître creuse*; and the largest and least subtle of all, *Crassotrea gigas*, the Pacific oyster. This is also the hardiest and fastest-growing oyster, and dominates the production in the Bay of Arcachon.

Oysters are graded according to size, either on a scale of 0 to 6, the largest being 0, or, as at the Marché des Capucins, by grades in the form of acronyms, from TP (*toutes petites*), through to G (*grosses*) and even TG (*très grosses*), the largest. Here, there are oysters not only from Cap-Ferret in the Bay of Arcachon, but also the prized green-tinged *vertes de Marennes*, and even some all the way from Brittany, which are the most expensive.

In the pleasantly scruffy seaside town of Pauillac, better known for its fine wine than its seafood, you can buy freshly boiled shrimps and wander along the *quai*, eating them from a paper cornet. Jean-Claude and Jean-Christophe Huguet are professional fishermen, whose patch lies towards the mouth of the Gironde estuary, where fresh water meets salt. As well as brown shrimps, *crevettes grises*, from the sea, they catch tiny, very pale pink shrimps, *crevettes blanches*, from the salt-fresh waters of the estuary, and these are the sweetest of all. Delicately flavoured with star anise, they are tender enough to eat unpeeled, with only the heads and tails removed. Being estuary fishermen, the Huguets also catch migratory fish: lamprey in February and March, and shad in May and June, which the female members of the family sell at local markets. Paul Héraud is another fisherman, now in semi-retirement, who opens up his lovely, old-fashioned shop on the seafront when the mood takes him, to sell the day's catch of shrimps, grey mullet and sole.

The production of Gironde caviar started after the First World War, when Monsieur Prunier (of the famous Paris restaurant) travelled to the region and, noticing how much sturgeon was eaten there, spotted an opportunity for producing caviar. Preserved with far less salt than the

ABOVE On the waterfront at Pauillac, Paul Héraud sells pink shrimps, freshly-boiled and sweet-tasting. LEFT AND FAR LEFT Some of the paraphernalia of oyster-farming, including (left) the racks where whitewashed terracotta tiles will be placed, to which the tiny oysters attach themselves. Here they stay, submerged by the sea twice a day, until they are big enough to go out to parks in the bay.

HAUT-MEDOC
CHATEAU
SOCIANDO-MALLET

Lying on the banks of the Gironde, this old estate
of large rolling vineyards covers some of the
finest land in the Médoc. Wine has been made
here since the early 17th century, but it was
not until 1969, after the property had been
bought by Jean Gautreau, that Sociando-
Mallet began to establish a reputation which
ranks it among the élite of crus bourgeois wines.
A classic wine of the Haut-Médoc, Château
Sociando-Mallet is intensely aromatic, with
scents of vanilla and cedarwood. The
overwhelming character of the wine is
dominated by the blackcurrant flavours of
Cabernet Sauvignon. Characteristically
tough and tannic in their youth, these wines
are slow to mature, but develop well
and age superbly.

ABOVE RIGHT Plantings of young vines at
Château Lafite, in the north of the commune of
Pauillac. The chateau itself is hidden by trees.

Russian version, it was best eaten very fresh, and was highly prized. Gironde caviar, which once accounted for one-quarter of all caviar consumed in France, is no longer made from the wild fish, as the latter is almost extinct.

Sturgeon are huge, powerful fish, with shovel-like snouts and rows of bony protuberances along their length. Their flesh is said to taste like veal. Much sought after during the early years of the century, mostly for caviar, the wild sturgeon was at that time a common fish. But by 1980, the Gironde, Garonne and Dordogne were the only rivers in Europe still to contain sturgeon, and even there, stocks were dramatically reduced, due to over-fishing and the extraction of gravel from the river. In 1982, it became illegal to catch them, but sadly, it remains an endangered species; indeed, it looks as if this noble fish will soon become extinct in European waters, because poachers continue to defy the law.

THE WINES OF THE BORDELAIS

Centred on the valleys of three rivers – the Dordogne, the Garonne, and their shared estuary, the Gironde – the Bordelais is possibly the most celebrated, most complicated and most variable fine wine region in the world. With a temperate climate, typically damp in spring and sunny in autumn, it is a region of gently sloping hills inclined towards the sun and mainly gravelly soils, which provide perfect conditions for the vine to flourish. No other wine-producing region in the world can claim such variety in its wines, which range in quality from the very finest to the most humble; in style from deep, rich reds to luscious dessert wines, from rosy pink *clairets* to steely dry whites. There are even sparkling wines, both white and rosé. With such natural riches it is easy to forget, however, that the wines are ultimately the result of the efforts of the *viticulteurs* – the winemakers – who put into practice techniques learnt during the region's long history of research and development. Work carried out at the University of Bordeaux's department of oenology and other research institutes gives rise to constant refinement of techniques, both in viticulture and in vinification.

Wine-making has a long history in the Bordelais – the scholar-poet Ausonius recorded the existence of vine-covered slopes in the fourth century AD – but a second-century inscription suggests that the city of Bordeaux was exporting wine even before vines were planted there by the Romans. Right from the start, it was the British who were the keenest customers, and centuries later, trading links between Bordeaux and Britain were further strengthened by the marriage in 1152 of Eleanor of Aquitaine to Henry Plantagenet, heir to the English throne. As a result, Eleanor's vast possessions in south-west France became subject to British rule, and remained so for 300 years. During this time the English thirst for Bordeaux *clairet*, as the light red wines were then known, became a habit that would last a very long time. (The word *clairet* now describes the deep rosé wines of the Bordelais, while claret has come to mean red Bordeaux to the English-speaking world.)

In the early days, the wines were exported in barrels before Christmas in the year of production, and consumed before the next vintage, because no way had been found of preserving them, but by the beginning of the eighteenth century, English entrepreneurs were buying young Bordelais wines, bottled and sealed, for ageing. This was to be the beginning of the notion of quality, of the relationship between the chateau and its wine, and by the end of the century, the hierarchy of *crus bordelais* had been established.

THE 1855 CLASSIFICATION

The wines of the Médoc and Graves were first officially classified in 1855, when the four chateaux considered to produce the finest wine – Margaux, Lafite, Latour and Haut-Brion – were put in a class of their own: *premier cru classé* or first growth. Mouton-Rothschild was added to this list in 1973. A further 58 chateaux were classified as second, third, fourth and fifth growths, although today, EC labelling regulations recognize only first and second growths; the third, fourth and fifth are simply labelled *cru classé*. Considered to be below *grand cru* status, but nonetheless recognized for their excellence, are wines labelled *cru bourgeois*. The wines of Sauternes were also classified in 1855, with 11 *premiers crus*, and one *premier cru supérieur*, Château d'Yquem, ranked above even the greatest wines of the Médoc.

The order of this official list was determined by a syndicate of brokers for the Paris International Exhibition. Surprisingly, the classification was not based on a blind tasting, or on the past reputation of the growers; it was assessed simply by the price the wines were then fetching on the open market. As such, it probably provided a convenient price guideline for the trade, rather than a quality guide for connoisseurs. Over the years, the 1855 classification has been widely criticized for being outdated and inflexible, but for all its shortcomings it has survived, and it arguably gives the layman a fair picture of the relative standing of the élite of Bordeaux estates.

GRAND ENCLOS DU CHATEAU DE CERONS

On the left bank of the Garonne, adjoining Barsac, is the small wine area of Cérons. At one time it used to be part of Sauternes, and it produces wines of a similar style, though less sweet. The vines, planted on sandy, gravelly soils, are Sémillon, Sauvignon Blanc and Muscadelle, and are sometimes affected by botrytis ('noble rot'), which is responsible for wonderful honeyed flavours in the wine.

For those who enjoy sweet wines but find Sauternes too rich or too expensive, Cérons is an excellent alternative and not too well known by consumers. One of the best properties is Olivier Lataste's Grand Enclos du Château de Cérons, entirely enclosed by walls, and situated in the very centre of the village. The wine produced there has an elegant bouquet, and is powerful yet delicate at the same time, with a long finish – a sure sign of a well-made, mature wine.

LA ROUTE DES VINS

The small D2 road that leads north out of Bordeaux may not look much on the map, but for wine connoisseurs it is the ultimate journey. As the route winds through small villages and dense vineyards, it takes you through several of the world's most famous estates and a succession of opulent chateaux: the neo-classical Palmer, the monumental Ducru-Beaucaillou and the extravagantly oriental Cos d'Estournel.

As the road runs northwards, along a narrow 98-kilometre strip of land towards the mouth of the Gironde estuary, signposts point towards villages at the heart of the four great appellations of the Médoc: Margaux, Saint-Julien, Pauillac and Saint-Estèphe. There is an old saying in Médoc that the best quality wine is made within sight of the river, and it is true that four of the *premiers crus* estates, Châteaux Lafite, Latour, Margaux and Mouton-Rothschild, lie close to the banks of the Gironde, in a narrow band of land no more than four kilometres wide, which is renowned for its exceptionally favourable microclimate and soil.

Although not particularly fertile, the gravelly Médoc soils provide good drainage and also retain heat from the sun so the grapes continue to ripen by night; for this reason, the vines are pruned low, so as to get the maximum benefit from the warmth of the pebbles.

The great wines of the Bordelais can be divided into three categories: the red wines of the Médoc, Saint-Emilion, Pomerol and Fronsac, which at their best are unquestionably superlative; the dry white wines of the Graves, which can be very good but are rarely exceptional; and the sweet white wines of Sauternes and Barsac, which are of outstanding quality.

ABOVE A distant view of vineyards, seen over the terracotta rooftops of Saint-Emilion.
BELOW Amidst a sea of vines, the ancient chartreuse of Château Saint-Georges, in Saint-Georges Saint-Emilion, looms up majestically.

THE RED WINES

The red wines of the Médoc are noted for their intense colour, pronounced flavour and lingering finish. They are relatively low in alcohol, and as they are often very tannic, are capable of ageing superbly. At its best with food, a good claret must be one of the most elegant wines in the world.

The traditional grape blend in the Médoc is dominated by the blackcurrant-flavoured Cabernet Sauvignon; after that comes plummy Merlot, which is less tannic and therefore matures more quickly, and then Cabernet Franc. The finest wines bear the names of individual communes in the Haut-Médoc, for example AC Pauillac or Margaux, and will probably include the name of the chateau as well.

On the right bank of the Dordogne lie the regions of Pomerol and Saint-Emilion, centred on the picturesque medieval town of Saint-Emilion. The vineyards spread out over limestone hills, clustered around pretty chateaux and sleepy villages. The wines are rounder and more instantly appealing, having less tannin and a greater proportion of Merlot grapes in the blend. The superstars of Saint-Emilion are comparable in quality, and price, to the great growths of the Médoc, but they were only classified in 1955. Unlike the 1855 classification, this one is regularly reviewed. There are 11 *premier grand cru classé* properties, of which two, Château Ausone and Château Cheval Blanc, are considered in a class of their own.

ST-EMILION CHATEAU ROLLAND-MAILLET

A Saint-Emilion grand cru classé, *situated near the outer limit of the appellation, Château Rolland-Maillet belongs to husband-and-wife team Michel and Dany Rolland, who also own another property, Château Le Bon Pasteur, in neighbouring Pomerol. Both are oenologists; Michel is a superstar-winemaker, who sells his skills as far away as Argentina and California.*

The wine contains no Cabernet Sauvignon, one of the region's most characteristic grapes, but a high proportion of Merlot – about 85 per cent, the rest of the blend being Cabernet Franc. Long oak-ageing contributes to the complex bouquet and spicy intensity of the wine, which has all the delicious appeal of a rich, plummy fruitcake.

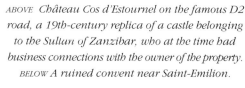

ABOVE *Château Cos d'Estournel on the famous D2 road, a 19th-century replica of a castle belonging to the Sultan of Zanzibar, who at the time had business connections with the owner of the property.* BELOW *A ruined convent near Saint-Emilion.*

RIGHT *During the harvest, grape-pickers lunch with the family in the old-fashioned kitchen at Château de Landiras, in the Graves region. A rustic dish of baked pumpkin stuffed with lentils is washed down with their own red wine.*

LEFT AND BELOW *Vines growing in the region of Sauternes, a small enclave within the Graves district. Dense early morning mists rolling across the vineyards of Sauternes encourage the growth of botrytis or 'noble rot', a fungus, beneficial to wine producers, which causes grapes to shrivel up and the sugar within to become concentrated.*

Dotted around Saint-Emilion are the 'satellites', which have the right to link their names with Saint-Emilion, such as Lussac Saint-Emilion or Puisseguin Saint-Emilion. The grape varieties are the same, and at their best, these wines can approach those of their namesake in quality. Pomerol has no classification of its own. Its wines are long-lived, rich and powerful, made primarily from ripe, plummy Merlot grapes. Its best property is Château Pétrus, considered to be on a par with the greatest *premiers crus* of the Médoc. Less well known, and less expensive, are the wines of nearby Fronsac – heavy, meaty wines which can be very good, especially if mellowed by being aged in bottle for a few years.

THE DRY WHITE WINES

On the left bank of the River Garonne is the vast region of Graves, where the best dry white wines of the Bordelais are produced. Elegant and full, the wines are made from Sauvignon Blanc grapes, with their aroma of gooseberries, supplemented by the richness of Sémillon and a touch of Muscadelle; they are often matured in oak *barriques*, which gives them richness and complexity. The region also produces excellent red wines, including those of Château Haut-Brion, listed in 1855 with the finest growths of the Médoc.

THE GOLDEN SWEET WINES

Within the Graves region lie the sweet wine-producing districts of Sauternes and Barsac, where the moist, misty microclimates encourage the development of *botrytis* or 'noble rot', which shrivels the ripe grapes and concentrates the sugar. It is this concentration of sugar and flavour that results in the rich, luscious sweet wines for which the region is so well known. Made from Sémillon, Sauvignon Blanc and Muscadelle grapes, these complex *vins liquoreux* are often considered purely as dessert wines, but in this part of France they are also served as an aperitif, or to accompany foie gras. Sweet wine is, incidentally, the perfect partner for salty blue cheese, such as roquefort. Most famous of all, of course, is Château d'Yquem.

CHEAP AND CHEERFUL

While Bordeaux is most famous for its expensive, top-quality wines, it is also a region where a vast quantity of wine is produced, of all styles and at all prices. In the race to keep up with changing tastes, there is a move towards the making of crisp, dry, white wines from the Sauvignon Blanc grape, especially in the Entre-Deux-Mers region, as well as in Blaye, Côte de Bourg and Graves. Sparkling *crémant de Bordeaux* and *mousseux* wines can be highly drinkable, too, as can the fresh and fruity *clairet* – deeper in colour than rosé, and perfect for summer lunches. Sweet wines of very high quality offer good value for money, and if Sauternes prices seem high, try Sainte-Croix-du-Mont or Loupiac for less expensive rivals.

ABOVE *In between the vineyards, the sandy gravel soils of the Graves support vast areas of pine forest, planted for timber, resin, turpentine and paper pulp. This monotonous landscape extends westwards to the Landes, where pine trees take over completely.*

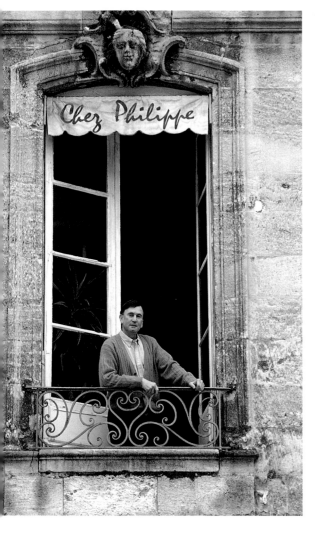

CHEZ PHILIPPE

BORDEAUX, TEL 56 81 83 15

Kings and queens, sailors and fishermen, office workers and tourists make up the cosmopolitan clientèle at Chez Philippe, Bordeaux's best-loved fish restaurant. Philippe Téchoire's father was a fisherman, and his mother, Irène, was an excellent cook, who ran a seaside restaurant in Le Canon and handed on her skills to her son. In 1968, he opened Chez Philippe, and little has changed since, except that it has become something of an institution in the city of Bordeaux.

Fish and shellfish of impeccable freshness, cooked and served with the utmost simplicity, in an ambience which is completely unfussy and unpretentious, are the hallmarks of the restaurant. In season, there are pibales *(elvers), sautéd and seasoned with garlic, cayenne pepper and parsley;* carpaccio *(raw, wafer-thin slices) of fresh tuna; salads of red mullet and anchovies; baby cuttlefish cooked in their own ink; turbot, seabass, sole . . .*

PAPILLOTES DE CABILLAUD AUX HUITRES

Cod Steaks Baked with Oysters, Spinach, and Tomato

Philippe Téchoire's style of cooking is very simple – subtle but never extravagant – and depends on the absolute freshness and quality of the ingredients. This dish combines cod, an everyday fish yet one of the most delicious when really fresh, with a touch of luxury – oysters. (Illustrated right, above)

SERVES 4
4 cod steaks, each weighing about 200g/7oz
1 dozen oysters, size 3
55g/2oz butter
225g/8oz spinach, washed and with stalks removed
2 large tomatoes, peeled, deseeded and diced
4tbsp fish stock
salt and freshly ground black pepper
beurre blanc, to serve

Preheat the oven to 230°C/450°F/gas mark 8. Season the cod steaks with salt and pepper.

Open the oysters with a short, sharp knife. This is not difficult once the technique has been mastered. Place the oyster in one hand, convex side down, and starting from the pointed end, move two-thirds of the way towards the blunt end of the shell. The muscle that joins the two sides of the shell is here, so insert the knife, twist quickly, catching all of the oyster liquor, and detach each oyster from its shell.

Cut 4 rectangles of foil measuring approximately 30 x 46cm/12 x 18in, and butter the centre of each generously. Place on each piece of foil some of the spinach leaves and chopped tomato, a cod steak and 3 oysters with some of their juice, and a spoonful of fish stock. Season with salt and pepper. Dot the ingredients with the remaining butter, and fold up the foil envelopes to seal them.

Place on a baking sheet, and bake for 20 minutes. The spinach leaves will wilt, and the cod and oysters will yield a small amount of well-flavoured buttery juices.

Serve with beurre blanc, and plenty of crusty bread to mop up the sauce.

ORANGES ORIENTALES
Oriental Oranges

This refreshing dessert is one of the regular favourites at Chez Philippe, and is very simple and quick to make. The grenadine gives a wonderful colour. (Illustrated left, below)

SERVES 4
6 oranges
100g/3½oz caster sugar
1tbsp orange-flavoured liqueur, such as Cointreau
1tbsp grenadine or pomegranate juice
***tuiles d'amandes*, to serve**

Peel the zest thinly from 2 of the oranges, taking off as little pith as possible, and cut the zest into julienne strips. Blanch in boiling water for 1 minute, drain and refresh under cold water, then repeat the process. Next, cut the 2 oranges in half, and squeeze out their juice. Put the orange juice to one side.

With a sharp knife, peel the remaining oranges, and cut into segments, leaving behind all pith and membrane.

Dissolve the sugar over gentle heat, to form a pale golden caramel, then carefully pour on the orange juice. It will splutter, and the caramelized sugar will quickly go solid, like toffee. Set it aside for a few minutes, stirring from time to time, until the toffee dissolves into the warm juice, then put back over gentle heat and simmer for a minute or so, until a light syrup is formed. Add the strips of orange zest, the Cointreau and grenadine to the syrup, and bring back to the boil, then take off the heat. Allow to cool.

To serve, arrange the orange slices together with the strips of zest on individual plates, pour sauce over, and offer *tuiles d'amandes* biscuits separately.

TARTES AUX TOMATES ET AU BASILIC

Tomato and Basil Tarts

In the quiet village of Sauternes, Evelyne Bialasik serves a perfect pairing of local wines and regional food at the rustic Auberge des Vignes. Foie gras, grillades aux sarments, *and* lamproies à la bordelaise *all make regular appearances on the red-and-white check tablecloths, as well as these little tomato and basil tarts, served with a light sauce of crème fraîche, shallots and lemon juice.*

SERVES 4
200g/7oz puff pastry
bunch of fresh basil leaves
100ml/3½fl oz olive oil
4 large, sweet tomatoes
salt and freshly ground black pepper

FOR THE SAUCE
150ml/5floz crème fraîche or whipping cream thickened with a squeeze of lemon juice
1 shallot, very finely chopped
salt and freshly ground black pepper

Preheat the oven to 220°C/425°F/gas mark 7. Cut out 4 circles of pastry, about 15cm/6in in diameter, prick with a fork, and place on a greased baking sheet. Keep them cool while you prepare the other ingredients.

In an electric blender, make a purée from the basil leaves and olive oil. Slice the tomatoes thinly, discarding the small rounds from either end. Spread a layer of basil purée on each pastry circle, to within 1cm/½in of the edge of each circle, and arrange the tomato slices on top so that they overlap. Spoon the remaining basil purée over the tomatoes and

season with salt and pepper. Bake the tarts in the oven for 5 minutes, then turn down the heat to 200°C/400°F/gas mark 6, for another 10–15 minutes.

Mix together the ingredients for the sauce, and serve the tarts warm, with the sauce poured over.

PATE DE LAPIN AU ROMARIN

Rabbit Pâté with Rosemary

This recipe also comes from Evelyne Bialasik, chef-patronne of L'Auberge des Vignes, in the village of Sauternes. As well as having a good flavour, it is very lean; it would be good served with a sweet onion relish or chutney.

SERVES 8–10
1 rabbit, boned (keep the bones)
2 garlic cloves, chopped
equal weight of fat bacon (about 700g/1⅔lb)
pinch of thyme, finely chopped
140g/5oz bacon rinds
1 carrot, peeled and sliced
4 sprigs fresh rosemary, finely chopped
salt and freshly ground black pepper

Ask the butcher to bone the rabbit, keeping the loins intact. Mince the rest of the meat, or chop it coarsely in a food processor. Add the garlic to the meat. Weigh the rabbit meat, and mince or chop an equal weight of fatty bacon. Mix with the rabbit, season with thyme, salt and pepper, and set aside. Do not over-salt, as the bacon is fairly salty.

Put the rabbit bones in a large pan, with the bacon rind, sliced carrot, and more thyme. Cover with water, and simmer for 2 hours.

During the last part of the cooking, remove the lid to allow the stock to become more concentrated. Add 500ml/16fl oz of the stock to the minced meats, and mix well. Preheat the oven to 190°C/375°F/gas mark 5.

Put half of the minced meats into the bottom of a 1½-litre/3-pint terrine, and lay the two whole loins lengthwise on top. Sprinkle with the rosemary. Cover with the remaining meat, seal the terrine with a lid or foil, and cook for 2 hours, taking off the lid for the last half hour to brown the top.

Leave to cool, then refrigerate. Serve the pâté in slices with toast or crusty bread.

SALADE D'AUTOMNE

Autumn Salad of Bayonne Ham, Pickled Pears and Salad Leaves

Bernard Lafon preserves a rare variety of pear, Sarteau Rouge, in sweet, spiced vinegar, and suggests this way of serving them. The pears he uses are quite small; larger fruit should be sliced. (Illustrated right)

SERVES 4
115g/4oz piece of streaky bacon, diced
115g/4oz each of rocket, corn salad, and frisée or chicory
200g/7oz pickled pears (350ml/12fl oz jar)
115g/4oz Bayonne ham, diced
55g/2oz shelled walnuts
walnut oil, for vinaigrette

Brown the bacon in a little oil. Make a vinaigrette with the walnut oil and a little of the vinegar from the pears, and toss the salad leaves in the dressing. Arrange the pears, diced bacon, ham and walnuts over the salad leaves. Serve immediately.

ARTICHAUTS FARCIS A LA PUREE D'ASPERGES

Artichokes Stuffed with a Purée of Asparagus

The countryside around Macau, on the Gironde estuary, is famous for globe artichokes, while Blaye across the Gironde has a reputation for its asparagus; the two are combined in this summery hors d'oeuvre. In her Vegetable Book *(1978), Jane Grigson provides an alternative suggestion as a stuffing for artichokes – broad bean purée flavoured with savory. (Illustrated on page 142)*

SERVES 4
4 globe artichokes
300g/10½oz green asparagus tips
55g/2oz butter
4 tbsp crème fraîche
chopped fresh parsley and chervil
lemon juice, to season
salt and freshly ground black pepper

Bring a large pan of salted water to the boil. Break the stalks off the artichokes, trim the bases and snip off the spiny leaf tips with scissors. With a sharp knife, remove the pointed ends of the artichokes, cutting parallel to the base. Simmer the artichokes in boiling water for 35–45 minutes, until the leaves can easily be pulled off. Drain them upside-down.

To make the purée, first trim the asparagus, cook for about 15 minutes, then drain. Blend to a rough purée with the remaining ingredients.

Remove the central core of leaves from each artichoke, scrape out the hairy choke with a teaspoon, and fill the hollow with purée. Serve warm. The leaves are pulled off one at a time, and used to scoop out some filling, then the heart is eaten with a knife and fork.

OIGNONS FARCIS

Stuffed Onions

The Bordelais is famous for its shallots, but onions, in all their colourful variety, are another speciality. Stalls at the Marché des Capucins in Bordeaux are piled high with bunches of purple, white and golden onions, sold in season with leaves still attached.

SERVES 6
6 large onions
100g/3½oz fat bacon, diced
225g/8oz mushrooms, sliced
2tbsp oil
100g/3½oz ham, diced
1tbsp chopped parsley
100g/3½oz white breadcrumbs
6tbsp milk
pinch of nutmeg
salt and freshly ground black papper

Cut roots and stems from the onions, and remove the outer skin. Bring a large pan of salted water to the boil, and simmer the onions, base down, for 50 minutes.

Preheat the oven to 200°C/400°F/gas mark 6.

Meanwhile, make the stuffing. Sauté the bacon and mushrooms in the oil, then stir in the ham and parsley. Soak the breadcrumbs in milk and squeeze out, then add to pan. Season to taste with salt, pepper and nutmeg.

When the onions are cooked, drain upside-down for a few minutes, then carefully cut a circle around the core at the base and push out the central layers of onion, leaving enough outside layers to hold the shell together. Chop the centres and add to the stuffing.

Stuff each onion with the filling, piling it up high, and place in a greased baking dish. Bake for about 50 minutes, or until well browned.

MOULES A LA BORDELAISE

Mussels Bordeaux-style

Mussels, as well as oysters, are raised in the Bay of Arcachon, and are cooked in many different ways. This is one of the classics, a first-course dish that is simple and quick to prepare. Some versions add one or two peeled and chopped tomatoes to the ham and breadcrumb mixture.

SERVES 2–3
1kg/2¼lb fresh mussels
4tbsp white wine
2 shallots, finely chopped
3 garlic cloves, finely chopped
55g/2oz air-dried ham, such as *jambon de Bayonne*, diced
45g/1½oz butter
2tbsp white breadcrumbs
3tbsp chopped parsley

Clean the mussels, pulling away the beards, and discarding any with broken shells or that do not close when tapped. In a large saucepan with a lid, steam them open, and strain the liquor into a smaller pan. Add the wine and reduce slightly over gentle heat.

Remove upper shell from each mussel, and discard, along with the rubbery ring around the shell. Place mussels in an ovenproof dish, and keep warm, covered with foil, in a low oven.

Sauté the shallots, garlic and ham in half of the butter, over low heat, but do not allow to brown. When shallots are soft, add the wine and mussel liquor, and bring back to the boil. Adjust seasoning, taking care not to over-salt. Stir in the breadcrumbs and parsley. Add the remaining butter in small pieces, and stir around to distribute it evenly. Spoon over the mussels, and serve with crusty bread.

HUITRES CHAUDES

Baked Oysters with Shallots, Garlic and Parsley

The Bay of Arcachon is one of France's most important centres of ostréiculture, *and throughout the whole region, market stalls selling* hûitres *are a familiar sight. (Illustrated left)*

SERVES 4
30g/1oz butter
4 shallots, finely chopped
2 garlic cloves, finely chopped
3tbsp white wine
2tbsp chopped parsley
24 oysters
4tbsp grated gruyère
freshly ground black pepper

Preheat the oven to 220°C/425°F/gas mark 7. Melt the butter in a saucepan over medium heat, and cook the shallots and garlic for about 5 minutes, then add the wine and parsley and let the mixture bubble gently for another 2 minutes. Season with pepper, but do not add salt. Turn off the heat.

Open the oysters with a short, sharp knife: place the oyster in one hand, convex side down, and starting from the pointed end, move the knife two-thirds of the way towards the blunt end of the shell. The muscle that joins the two sides of the shell is here, so insert the knife, and twist quickly. Open the shell, draining away the seawater inside, and discarding the flat half-shell. Set the oysters on a bed of salt in a large baking tin; alternatively, wedge the oysters together so that they don't tip over. Spoon a little of the shallot and parsley mixture into each half-shell and top with grated cheese.

Bake in the oven for about 10 minutes, then serve immediately, with crusty bread.

LOTTE AUX BLETTES

Monkfish Baked with Swiss Chard and Mushrooms

If you ask a Bordelais to recommend a fish restaurant in Bordeaux, the chances are that he or she will suggest Chez Philippe (see pages 134–5). This recipe for baked monkfish comes from the patron, Philippe Téchoire. (Illustrated left)

SERVES 6
1.35kg/3lb monkfish
450g/1lb Swiss chard
55g/2oz butter
225g/7oz smoked bacon, diced
200g/7oz mushrooms, sliced
4 tomatoes, peeled, deseeded and chopped
salt and freshly ground black pepper
fresh chives and parsley, to garnish

Prepare the fish, stripping away all grey membrane, and cutting into steaks about 2cm/¾in thick. Strip leaves from chard, wash and set aside. (The leaves can be cooked separately, like spinach, and served, chopped and mixed with a little béchamel sauce and grated cheese, as an accompaniment to the finished dish.) Trim the chard stems, stripping off any tough fibres, and cut lengthwise into strips 1cm/½in across. Slice the strips into 5cm/2in batons.

In a large sauté pan, melt the butter, and over gentle heat, cook the bacon and chard batons for 15 minutes, until the chard is quite soft. Add the mushrooms, and cook for another 5 minutes, then add the monkfish and tomatoes. Season with salt and pepper, taking care not to over-salt (because of the bacon), cover and cook gently for another 15–20 minutes. Sprinkle with the chopped parsley and snipped chives, and serve, with the cooked chard leaves on the side.

ALOSE GRILLEE AUX SARMENTS

Shad Grilled over Vine Cuttings

A member of the herring family, shad is a migratory fish, which swims up the river to spawn in late spring. The flesh is delicate, but shad is full of tiny bones, which are a nuisance. Ask the fishmonger to clean and scale the fish, but to give you the roe, which is a delicacy. It can be placed on the barbecue grill towards the end of the cooking time.

SERVES 4
1 shad, weighing about 1.5kg/3½lb

FOR THE MARINADE
1 glass olive oil
1 glass white wine
2 or 3 bay leaves
several sprigs of parsley
1 small onion, minced
salt and freshly ground black pepper

FOR THE SAUCE
6tbsp olive oil
1tbsp wine vinegar
chopped fresh parsley, tarragon and chives
1 shallot, finely chopped
salt and freshly ground black pepper

Cover the fish with the marinade mixture, inside and out, and leave for at least an hour, turning over several times.

Prepare the fire half an hour before you plan to start cooking. It should have an even heat, and not be too hot. The cooking time will vary according to the size of the fish, but will probably be about 45 minutes. During this time the fish should be turned several times, and basted with the marinade.

To make the *sauce verte*, simply blend the ingredients as for a vinaigrette, and spoon it over the cooked portions of fish at table. Sorrel purée is also a good accompaniment.

CHIPIRONS SAUTES

Sautéed Baby Squid with Garlic and Parsley

Bordeaux's noisy Marché des Capucins is a daily event, held in a rather depressing space beneath a concrete car park. But the range and quality of the produce on sale is spectacular, especially the seafood, which sparkles with freshness out of the gloom. Baby squid is just one of the specialities, and it is particularly delicious cut into rings and fried.

SERVES 4
450g/1lb baby squid
2–3tbsp seasoned flour
2 garlic cloves, finely chopped
2 tbsp parsley, finely chopped
oil, for frying

Pull out the insides of each squid, which are attached to the head. Remove the plastic-like quill and any soft white innards and discard. Remove the purple skin from the outside of the body, and cut off the tentacles just above the eyes. Keep the tentacles, as they are edible. Slice each squid into rings.

Put some seasoned flour into a bowl, and heat some oil for frying.

When the oil is hot, dredge the squid pieces with flour, shake off excess, and fry until brown and crisp. You will probably have to do this in batches. Drain on paper towels and strew with garlic and parsley. Serve as a starter with lemon wedges.

PARFAIT GLACE AU SAUTERNES

Iced Sauternes Parfait

At the Auberge du Vignes in the village of Sauternes, Evelyne Bialasik naturally uses the luscious sweet wine in many different ways, one of which is this delicious parfait glacé. *Prepare it one day in advance. (Illustrated above, right)*

SERVES 8–10
10 eggs
450g/1lb caster sugar
1 bottle Sauternes

500ml/16fl oz crème fraîche
or whipping cream

Separate the eggs, and put 3 of the whites in a bowl large enough to whisk them later.

In another bowl, whisk all of the egg yolks with 400g/14oz of the sugar, until pale and creamy. Bring the Sauternes to the boil in a saucepan, and add it to the yolks, whisking constantly, then pour it all back into the pan. Over very gentle heat, warm the liquid, still stirring, and taking care not to let the mixture boil, until it thickens enough to coat the back of a wooden spoon. Strain and allow to cool.

Meanwhile, whisk the 3 egg whites until stiff, then whisk in the remaining sugar, a teaspoon at a time. In another bowl, lightly whip the cream with another spoonful of sugar.

Blend the cream with the cooled egg yolks mixture, then carefully fold in the stiff egg whites, trying to keep the mixture as light as possible. Freeze in an ice-cream maker if you have one or turn into a metal container lined with silicone paper, and freeze for about 5 hours or more. Remove from the freezer about half an hour before serving.

Serve with sliced white peaches (which have a better flavour than yellow ones) or other fresh fruit, together with almond biscuits, and a glass of chilled Sauternes.

CANNELES DE BORDEAUX

Bordeaux Cakes

The small, sweet cakes known as cannelés *were first baked in Bordeaux by nuns at the convent next to the Church of Divine Mercy, who were nicknamed '*les filles au corset rouge*', because of their colourful habits. The flour was apparently scoured from the holds of ships in the old port. After the revolution,* cannelés *began to be baked by local pâtissiers, and now they are a famous Bordeaux speciality.*

The cakes are baked in fluted, dome-shaped moulds, which look a bit like miniature jelly moulds, and can be bought at hardware shops in Bordeaux. (Illustrated on page 125)

MAKES 12
55g/2oz butter, plus 30g/1oz for greasing
500ml/16fl oz milk
2 eggs and 1 egg yolk, beaten together
225g/8oz icing sugar
125g/4½oz flour
1 sachet vanilla sugar or few drops vanilla essence

Melt the 55g/2oz butter over very low heat. Warm the milk and pour over the eggs. Whisk well, and put back over a very low heat for another 5 minutes, continuing to stir with a wooden spoon, but do not allow to boil.

In a basin, mix the icing sugar with the sifted flour, and pour on the egg-and-milk mixture, stirring constantly. Add melted butter and vanilla, strain, and chill for several hours.

When ready to cook, preheat the oven to 190°C/375°F/gas mark 5. Using a pastry brush, grease the moulds generously with melted butter, then chill them for a few minutes (to set the butter), and dust with flour and icing sugar.

Stir the batter a few times and pour into the moulds, taking care not to fill them completely – they should be about two-thirds full. Place the moulds on a baking sheet, and put it into the hot oven. Bake for about 40 minutes, or until a skewer inserted into the centre comes out clean. Unmould the *cannelés* and leave to cool. They are best eaten the same day.

MACARONS

Macaroons

The wine town of Saint-Emilion is proud of its local speciality, small almond macaroons, sold in blue-and-white boxes containing several layers of six biscuits, baked on sheets of white paper. They have the distinctive flavour of bitter almonds. (Illustrated opposite)

MAKES 16
2 egg whites
100 g/3½oz caster sugar
115g/4oz ground almonds
1tbsp rice flour
few drops essence of bitter almonds
16 halves of blanched almonds
rice paper

Preheat the oven to 150°C/300°F/gas mark 2. Place rice paper on two baking sheets.

Whisk the egg whites until stiff, then gently fold in the sugar, ground almonds, rice flour and almond essence. Mix thoroughly, then place teaspoons of the mixture on to the rice paper, spacing them evenly and allowing space to spread a little. Put half an almond on each, then bake for about 15–20 minutes, until a pale golden brown. Allow to cool on a wire rack.

They are good to nibble after dinner, with coffee, or with a glass of dessert wine.

ST-EMILION AU CHOCOLAT

Chocolate and Macaroon Terrine

Saint-Emilion macaroons, soaked in rum, are used to make this delicious chocolate terrine. It is sinfully rich, and a little goes a long way.

SERVES 8–10
125g/4½oz butter
125g/4½oz caster sugar
2 egg yolks
150ml/5fl oz double cream
225g/8oz bitter chocolate
16–20 macaroons
5–6tbsp rum or brandy
whipped cream, to serve

Soften the butter, and cream it together with the sugar. In a separate bowl, whisk the egg yolks into the double cream. In a basin set over a pan of simmering water, melt the chocolate and blend with the egg and cream mixture, still over the heat. Stir for a few minutes to cook the egg yolks and thicken the chocolate cream, then take off the heat and allow to cool slightly. Beat into the butter and sugar mixture, working until smooth.

Break each macaroon into 3 or 4 rough pieces, and place in a bowl. Sprinkle with the rum or brandy, and leave for a few minutes to absorb the liquid, turning a few times.

Line the bottom of a 900g/2lb loaf tin or terrine with greaseproof paper, and arrange a layer of the macaroons in the bottom. Pour over a layer of chocolate cream, so that it covers the macaroons. Continue building up layers until all of the macaroons and chocolate are used up, then chill for 12 hours. Turn out on to a plate, and serve in thin slices, either on its own or with unsweetened, whipped cream.

A VISITOR'S GUIDE

This guide draws from the long list of restaurants, farms, markets and shops that we visited while researching this book. It is inevitably a personal selection, but provides a number of recommendations in all of the areas covered in the five chapters. Restaurants range from very grand, Michelin-starred establishments, where both food, service and decoration is of a very high standard, to down-to-earth *bistrots* and *ferme-auberges*, where the surroundings may be quite basic, but which are worth a visit for the home cooking.

The addresses listed here have been divided into three categories, marked with one, two or three asterisks (see below); these do not represent Michelin stars, but the degree of refinement to be found at each restaurant paralleled, more often than not, by the price. All offer regional dishes: when planning to eat in a *ferme-auberge* or simple country restaurant, it is worthwhile telephoning ahead to discuss the menu because many authentic local dishes take a long time to prepare, and must therefore be ordered the day before or earlier.

Restaurants are very good places to sample local wines, but for home consumption undoubtedly the best way to buy wine is to visit the producers and buy direct. Most welcome customers during normal working hours to taste and buy. Some are happy to show impromptu visitors around the property as well, but it is probably best to arrange this in advance. In the Bordelais appointments must almost invariably be made beforehand, so it is important to telephone ahead. There are exceptions, though, and the chateaux listed in the Bordelais section which are not marked with warnings about making prior arrangements are open to visitors in the normal way, as are all of the other vineyards listed in the regions of Cahors and Bergerac.

Some producers sell their wine *en vrac* for the customer to bottle himself, and this is an excellent way of buying wine for everyday consumption. Plastic containers holding 5, 10 or 15 litres are usually available for purchase at the winery for a few extra francs; otherwise, take your own containers and get them filled up from the vat. If kept cool and bottled within a few days, the wine should keep for a year or so.

Key to symbols used in this Guide:
- ••• A sophisticated restaurant, often with a Michelin star
- •• Value-for-money bourgeois cooking
- • A simply country inn or city bistro, where one can eat for about £10.00 per head.

PERIGORD NOIR

Restaurants

LA MEYNARDIE••
Paulin
Salignac
Tel 53 28 85 98

LE VIEUX LOGIS•••
Trémolat
Tel 53 22 80 06 (page 28)

AUBERGE LA GABARRE•
Saint-Julien-de-Lampon
Near Carlux
Tel 53 29 85 69
(on river Dordogne)

HOTEL-RESTAURANT CAYRE•
Rouffilhac
Carlux
Tel 53 29 70 24
(on river Dordogne)

HOTEL DU PONT•
Grolejac
Tel 53 28 15 94 (page 108)
(on river Dordogne)

RESTAURANT DE LA FERME•
Chez Escalier
Caudon-de-Vitrac
Montfort-Caudon
Tel 53 28 33 35

HOTEL DE L'ESPLANADE••
Domme
Tel 53 28 31 41
(view down to river Dordogne)

RELAIS DES 5 CHATEAUX••
Vézac
Tel 53 30 30 72

HOTEL-RESTAURANT LES
PECHEURS•
Le Bourg
Badefols-sur-Dordogne
Tel 53 22 50 31
(on river Dordogne)

MANOIR D'HAUTEGENTE•••
Coly en Périgord
Terrasson
Tel 53 51 68 03

CHATEAU DE PUY ROBERT•••
Montignac
Tel 53 91 92 13

LE CENTENAIRE•••
Les Eyzies-de-Tayac
Tel 53 06 97 18

CRO-MAGNON•••
Les Eyzies-de-Tayac
Tel 53 06 97 06

LE CENTRE••
Les-Eyzies-de-Tayac
Tel 53 06 97 13

RESTAURANT SAINT-ALBERT••
10 avenue du General Leclerc
Sarlat-la-Canéda
Tel 53 59 01 09

LABORDERIE••
Tamniès
Tel 53 29 68 59

BELVEDERE DE BELVES••
1 avenue Paul Crampel
Belvès
Tel 53 29 90 50

CHEZ SYLVESTRE•
Bouzic, Domme
Tel 53 28 41 01

FERME DU DUBOIS•
Peynègre, La Dornac
Tel 53 51 04 24

FERME-AUBERGE COUSTATY•
Fort de la Rhonie
Lieu-dit Boyer, Meyrals
Saint Cyprien
Tel 53 29 24 83

LES VOYAGEURS••
Beaumont
Tel 53 22 39 12

Information

The booklet 'Bienvenue à la Ferme
en Périgord' can be obtained
from the Chamber of Agriculture
in Périgueux and tourist offices.

Places of interest

MUSEE-AQUARIUM DE SARLAT
3 rue du Commandant Maratuel
Sarlat
Tel 53 59 44 58

MAISON DU CHATAIGNIER,
MARRONS ET CHAMPIGNONS
Syndicat d'Initiative
Villefranche-du-Périgord
Tel 53 29 98 37

Specialities of the region

MOULIN DE LA TOUR
(walnut oil)
Sainte-Nathalène
Sarlat
Tel 53 59 22 08

DISTILLERIE LA SALAMANDRE
(fruit liqueurs, eaux de vie)
Les Tissanderies
Sarlat
Tel 53 59 10 00

BOUCHERIE LAMBERT
(air-dried ham)
Domme
Tel 53 28 31 55

RIGHT ABOVE *The rooftops of Belvès, a
medieval hilltop village in
Périgord Noir.*
RIGHT *Urbain Tache, the miller at
Le Moulin de la Tour in
Sainte-Nathalène, where walnut oil
is made as well as flour.*

LALANDE

(*traiteur*, charcuterie, *tourtières*, *miques*)

36 avenue Gambetta

Sarlat

Tel 53 59 03 44

BAZIN

(walnut tart, chocolates)

22 avenue de la République

Sarlat

Tel 53 59 01 30

LOU PERIGORD

(fruit liqueurs and eaux-de-vie, chocolate-covered walnuts)

4 rue de la Liberté

Sarlat

Tel 53 59 00 34

FRANCIS AND MARTINE BORTOLIN

(goats' cheese)

Le Meynat, Carvès

Tel 53 29 06 87

BOULANGERIE DE LA GARE

(sourdough country bread)

avenue Madrazes

Sarlat

Tel 53 59 37 13

RENE NEUVILLE

(artisan baker)

Valeille

La Casagne, Terrasson

Tel 53 51 04 24

RENE CARRIER

(walnuts, green walnut jam, confit de noix, walnut oil)

Molières

Tel 53 22 51 40

DOMAINE DE BARBE

(foie gras, confit etc.)

Badefols-sur-Dordogne

Tel 53 22 52 19

ROGER CROUZEL

(foie gras, confit etc.)

Le Temple

Salignac

Tel 53 28 80 83

DOMAINE DE BEQUIGNOL

(fruit liqueurs and eaux-de-vie; chocolate-covered walnuts)

Carlux

Tel 53 29 73 41

COOPERATIVE SARLAT-PERIGORD

(foie gras, raw goose meat, goose fat)

rue de l'Abattoir

Sarlat

Tel 53 30 28 79

FERME DUBOIS

(goose foie gras, confit etc, walnut oil)

Peynègre

Ladornac

Tel 53 51 04 24

Markets

Belvès : *Saturday*

Domme: *Thursday*

Issigeac: *Sunday*

Le Bugue: *Tuesday, Saturday*

Le Buisson: *Friday*

Montignac: *Wednesday*

Rouffignac: *Sunday*

Sarlat: *Wednesday, Saturday*

Saint Cyprien: *Sunday*

Terrasson: *Thursday*

Villefranche-du-Périgord: *Saturday*

PERIGORD BLANC

Restaurants

CHEZ MARCEL•

37 avenue de Limoges, Périgueux

Tel 53 53 13 43

AU PETIT CHEF•

5 place du Coderc, Périgueux

Tel 53 53 16 03

LE MOULIN DE L'ABBAYE•••

Brantôme

Tel 53 05 80 22 (page 52)

AU FIL DE L'EAU•

21 quai Bertin, Brantôme

Tel 53 05 73 65

AUBERGE DE LA TRUFFE••

Sorges

Tel 53 05 02 05

LA CHOUETTE GOURMANDE•

Saint-Front-sur-Nizonne

Nontron

Tel 53 56 14 70

CHATEAU DE VIEUX MAREUIL•••

Vieux-Mareuil

Tel 53 60 77 15

LE LION D'OR••

place de l'Eglise, Manzac-sur-Vern

Tel 53 54 28 09 (page 54)

LA GRANGE•

Jumilhac-le-Grand

Tel 53 52 50 07

BAR-RESTAURANT THIMON•

4 rue Achille Simon, Ribérac

Tel 53 90 05 42

LA PETITE AUBERGE•

Castagnol

Saint-Mayme-de-Pereyrol

Tel 53 04 00 54/53 54 71 78

RELAIS DE GABILLOU••

route de Périgueux, Mussidan

Tel 53 81 01 42

Places of interest

MUSEE DU PERIGORD

22 cours Tourney, Périgueux

Tel 53 53 16 42

MUSEE DES ARTS ET TRADITIONS POPULAIRES

Saint-Privat

Tel 53 91 22 87

MUSEE DU FOIE GRAS

(foie gras museum)

Syndicat d'Initiative, Thiviers

Tel 53 55 12 50

ECO-MUSEE DE LA TRUFFE

(truffle museum)

Sorges

Tel 53 05 90 11

MUSEE DES ARTS ET TRADITIONS POPULAIRES

(18th-century furnished town house)

2 rue Raoul Grassin, Mussidan

Tel 53 81 23 55

LEFT The pinnacles and domes of Périgueux's Saint-Front cathedral, which was virtually rebuilt in the 19th century.
BELOW Selecting vegetables in Périgueux market.
BOTTOM LEFT Sign giving details of the truffle market in Excideuil.
BOTTOM RIGHT The 16th-century Château de Losse at Thonac.

Specialities of the region

POISSONNERIE MODERNE (fish)
13 place du Coderc, Périgueux
Tel 53 08 00 70

MARCHAL & PAUTET
(patisserie, tea-room)
9 place de l'Hôtel de Ville
Périgueux
Tel 53 53 42 30

FERME DES MANDIES
(unpasteurised ewes' milk cheese)
La Lidoire, Saint-Martin-de-Gurçon
Tel 53 82 40 44

LA FROMAGERIE (cheese shop)
9 rue Limogeanne, Périgueux
Tel 53 08 41 22

MARCEL DEBORD
(walnut and hazelnut oil)
Rochevideau
La Chapelle-Faucher, Brantôme
Tel 53 54 81 42

DANIEL BIBIE
(duck foie gras, confit)
La Ferme du Fraysse, Vergt
Tel 53 46 70 05

FROMAGERIE DE LA TRAPPE
(cheese, fruit pastilles, jam)
Abbaye Notre-Dame de Bonne
Espérance, Echourgnac
Tel 53 80 36 43

JEAN-PIERRE BOISSEUIL
(charcuterie, *boudins aux châtaignes*)
Miallet-en-Périgord, La Coquille
Tel 53 62 84 07

JEAN-CLAUDE JARRY
(organic apple juice)
route de Saint-Saud, Miallet
Tel 53 62 84 54

PHILIPPE FRANCOIS
(apple and pear juice, cider)
Le Domaine Neuf, Firbeix
Tel 53 52 89 41

MICHEL PERRIER
(sourdough country bread)
20 route de Bergerac, Mussidan
Tel 53 81 29 78

PERIGORD-QUERCY FOIES GRAS
(raw duck liver, meat, duck fat)
Les Chatignolles
Route Nationale Eyzerac, Thiviers
Tel 53 62 37 37

Markets

Brantôme: *Friday*
Excideuil: *Thursday*
Hautefort: *Wednesday*
Jumilhac: *2nd and 4th Wednesdays*
Mareuil: *Tuesday*
Montpon-Monesterol: *Wednesday*
Mussidan: *Saturday*
Neuvic: *Tuesday, Saturday*
Nontron: *Saturday*
Périgueux: *Wednesday, Saturday*
Ribérac: *Friday*
Saint-Astier: *Thursday*
Saint-Alvère: *Monday*
Saint-Pardoux: *Saturday, Sunday*
Thenon: *Tuesday*
Thiviers: *Saturday*
Tocane-Saint-Apre: *Saturday*
Vergt: *Friday*
Villamblard: *Monday*

QUERCY

Restaurants

LE PONT DE L'OUYSSE••
Lacave
Tel 65 37 87 04

CHATEAU DE MERCUES•••
Cahors
Tel 65 20 00 01

RESTAURANT LE BALANDRE••
Hotel Terminus
5 avenue Ch de Freycinet
Cahors
Tel 65 30 01 97

HOSTELLERIE DE GOUJOUNAC•
Goujounac
65 36 68 67

LE LION D'OR•
Lalbenque
Tel 65 31 60 19

LE GINDREAU•••
Saint-Médard
Catus
Tel 65 36 22 27 (page 84)

LYCEE PROFESSIONEL HOTELIER
(Hotel school restaurant)
avenue Roger Couderc
Souillac
65 37 89 88

AU DEJEUNER DE SOUSCEYRAC••
Sousceyrac
Tel 65 33 00 56

HOSTELLERIE DE LA BOURIANE••
place Foirail, Gourdon
Tel 65 41 16 37

LA TERRASSE••
Lacapelle-Marival
Tel 65 40 80 07

AUBERGE DU SOMBRAL••
Saint-Cirq Lapopie
Tel 65 31 26 08

LA PELISSARIA••
Saint-Cirq Lapopie
Tel 65 31 25 14

LA PETITE AUBERGE•
Domaine de Saint-Géry
Lascabanes
Tel 65 31 82 51 (page 83)

HOSTELLERIE DU ROOY••
chemin de Labourdette par D661
Villeneuve-sur-Lot
Tel 53 70 48 48

LA TOQUE BLANCHE••
Pujols
Villeneuve-sur-Lot
Tel 53 49 00 30

Places of interest

MUSEE DE CUZALS
(open-air farm-museum with live
animals)
Sauliac-sur-Celé
Cabrerets
Tel 65 22 58 63

MAISON DE LA VIE RURALE
(museum of rural life)
Marsal
Monflanquin
Tel 53 41 90 19

MUSEE DU PRUNEAU
(prune museum and shop)
Domaine du Gabach
route Départementale 911
Granges-sur-Lot
Tel 53 84 00 69

Specialities of the Region

GILBERT CARNEJAC
(walnut bread, rye bread)
39 rue Wilson
Cahors
Tel 65 35 21 43

DELICES DU VALENTRE
(*coque de Cahors au cédrat*, patisserie)
21 boulevard Léon Gambetta
Cahors
Tel 65 35 09 86

GODARD
(foie gras, confit etc)
route de Salviac-Fumel
Gourdon
Tel 65 41 03 97

FERME LACOSTE
(cabécou)
Les Alix
Rocamadour
Tel 65 33 62 66

HUILERIE DU LAC DE DIANE
(walnut oil, walnuts)
Les Landes
Martel
Tel 65 37 30 69

SERGE LABORIE
(sourdough bread)
Labastide du Vert and Luzech
Tel 65 36 24 62

MOULIN DU CROS
(stoneground flour, walnut bread)
Montagnac-sur-Lède
Monflanquin
Tel 53 36 44 78

MOULIN DE VARAIRE
(walnut oil)
Limogne
Tel 65 31 52 34

SEGUR OBIER
(truffles, ceps, conserves)
Souillac
Tel 65 32 78 31

MAISON VIGOUROUS
(eau-de-vie de prunes)
9 place de la République
Gramat

CHIMERA
(English and French books,
secondhand and new)
Faubourg Saint-Privat
Montcuq
Tel 65 22 97 01

LEFT At Les Alix near Rocamadour, where cabécou goats' cheese is made.
ABOVE Saint-Cirq-Lapopie, perched on a rocky cliff above the river Lot.
RIGHT Romanesque domes of Souillac Abbey.

BOUTIQUE DES PRUNEAUX
(prunes, *crème de pruneaux*, eau-
de-vie)
Porte de Paris, Villeneuve-sur-Lot
Tel 53 70 02 75

LE COMPTOIR GOURMAND
(walnut oil, conserves, verjuice)
24 place Champollion
Cahors
Tel 65 23 97 66

FAVOLS
(jams, preserves, *pruneaux fourrés*)
Bias, Villeneuve-sur-Lot
Tel 53 40 15 15

PIERRE LAYE
(Quercy lamb and other meat)
Les Halles, Cahors
Tel 65 35 04 09

PONTHOREAU
(*jambon de Tonneins, boudins*)
8 rue du Maréchal Joffre
Tonneins
Tel 53 79 11 12

Markets

Agen: *Wednesday, Saturday*
Bretenoux: *Tuesday, Saturday*
Cahors: *Tuesday, Thursday, Saturday,*
Sunday
Gourdon: *Thursday* (marché fermier)
Gramat: *Friday*
Labastide-Murat: *Sunday* (marché
fermier)
Lalbenque (truffles): *Tuesday 2.30pm,*
Dec 1st–March 20th
Luzech: *Wednesday*
Marmande: *Saturday*
Martel: *Wednesday, Saturday*

Monflanquin: *Thursday*
Monsempron-Libos: *Thursday*
Penne d'Agenais: *Sunday*
Prayssac: *Friday*
Puy l'Eveque: *Thursday, Saturday*
Saint-Germain-du-Bel Air: *Sunday*
Sainte-Livrade-sur-Lot: *Friday*
Souillac: *Monday, Wednesday, Friday*
Tonneins: *Wednesday*
Villeneuve-sur-Lot: *Wednesday*
(organic); *Tuesday, Saturday*
Villeréal: *Saturday*

Vineyard visiting

CHATEAU DE HAUTE-SERRE
Cieurac
Tel 65 20 80 20

CLOS DE GAMOT
Prayssac
Tel 65 22 45 44

DOMAINE DES SAVARINES
Trespoux
Tel 65 22 33 67

LES COTES D'OLT
(cave coopérative)
Parnac, Luzech
Tel 65 30 71 86

CLOS LA COUTALE
Vire-sur-Lot
Tel 65 36 51 47

PRIEURE DE CENAC
Château de Saint-Didier-Parnac
Parnac
Tel 65 30 70 10

LEFT A peaceful scene on the river near Carennac.
ABOVE The Comte de Bosredon, of Château Belingard, Bergerac wine region.
RIGHT Statue of Cyrano de Bergerac.

BERGERACOIS

Restaurants

HOTEL-RESTAURANT DE LA POSTE••
Mauzac, Lalinde
Tel 53 22 50 52

HOTEL DU CHATEAU••
1 rue de Verdun, Lalinde
Tel 53 61 01 82

FERME-AUBERGE LA BARABIE•
D32 Lamonzie-Monastruc
Mouleydier, Nr Bergerac
Tel 53 23 22 47

LE CYRANO••
2 boulevard Montaigne, Bergerac
Tel 53 57 02 76

Places of interest

CHATEAU DE MONBAZILLAC
Monbazillac
Tel 53 57 06 38

MUSEE DE VIN ET DE LA
BATELLERIE
Bergerac
Tel 53 57 80 92

Specialities of the region

PAIN BIOLOGIQUE DES GALUBES
(Gilbert Bardone's organic bread)
Prigonrieux
Bergerac
Tel 53 57 59 18

POISSONNERIE RONNAT
5 place Jules Ferry, Bergerac
Tel 53 57 07 86

DOMAINE DE SIORAC
(verjuice)
Saint-Aubin-de-Cadelech
Eymet
Tel 53 24 50 76

BOUCHERIE BEAUFILS
(charcuterie)
route Sainte-Cathérine, Bergerac
Tel 53 57 01 66

PATISSERIE ROSIER
10 rue de la Résistance, Bergerac
Tel 53 57 04 42

DOMAINE DE CAZALS
(foie gras, confit)
Tiregand, Creysse, Bergerac
Tel 53 23 40 31

Markets

Bergerac: *Wednesday, Saturday*
Branne: *Thursday*
Castillon: *Monday*
Creysse: *Sunday*
Eymet: *Thursday*
Lalinde: *Thursday*
Prigonrieux: *Tuesday*
Sigoulès: *Friday*
Siorac: *Wednesday, Saturday* (*May-October*)
Sainte-Foy-La-Grande: *Saturday*

Vineyard visiting

BORDELAIS

CHATEAU BELINGARD
Pomport
Sigoulès
Tel 53 58 28 03

CHATEAU DE LA BORDERIE
Sigoulès
Monbazillac
Tel 53 57 00 36

CHATEAU DE LA JAUBERTIE
Colombier
Tel 53 58 32 11

CHATEAU COURT LES MUTS
Razac-de-Saussignac
Tel 53 27 92 17

CHATEAU DE PANISSEAU
Thénac
Tcl 53 58 40 03

CHATEAU LE RAZ
Saint-Méard-de-Gurçon
Tel 53 82 48 41

CHATEAU DE TIREGAND
Creysse
Bergerac
Tel 53 23 21 08

DOMAINE DU HAUT PECHARMANT
Pécharmant
Bergerac
Tel 53 57 29 50

CHATEAU RICHARD
La Croix Blanche
Monestier
Tel 53 58 49 13

Restaurants

LE CHAPON FIN•••
5 rue Montesquieu
Bordeaux
Tel 56 79 10 10

ST JAMES•••
3 place Camille Hostein
Bouliac, Bordeaux
Tel 56 20 52 19

JEAN RAMET•••
7 place Jean Jaurès
Bordeaux
Tel 56 44 12 51

RESTAURANT GRAVELIER••
114 cours de Verdun
Bordeaux
Tel 56 44 15 86

CHEZ PHILIPPE••
1 place du Parlement, Bordeaux
Tel 56 81 83 15 (page 134)

LA TUPINA••
6 rue Porte-de-la-Monnaie
Bordeaux
Tel 56 91 56 37

BRASSERIE DE NOAILLES••
12 allées de Tourny, Bordeaux
Tel 56 81 94 45

BISTROT DU SOMMELIER•
167 rue Georges Bonnac
Bordeaux
Tel 56 96 71 78

BAR DES CAPUCINS•
108 cours de la Marne
Bordeaux
Tel 56 91 36 47

LE BISTROT DE JOSEPH•
21 rue des Douves
Bordeaux
56 94 14 76

LE CELLIER BORDELAIS•
30 quai de la Monnaie
Bordeaux
Tel 56 31 30 30

CHEZ JOEL D, LE BISTROT DE
L'HUITRE•
13 rue des Piliers, Bordeaux
Tel 56 52 68 31

CHEZ MAZERE•
15 rue Marbotin
Bordeaux
Tel 56 31 38 30

LE CLARET•
46 rue du Pas Saint-Georges
Bordeaux
Tel 56 01 21 21

L'ECLUSE•
15 allées de Tourny
Bordeaux
Tel 56 81 49 94

AUBERGE DU MARAIS••
22 route de Lastresne
Bouliac, Bordeaux
Tel 56 20 52 17

AUBERGE DES VIGNES•
place de l'Eglise
Sauternes
Tel 56 63 60 06

AUBERGE DE LA FORET•
Salleboeuf
Tel 56 21 25 49

AUBERGE LE SAVOIE••
Margaux
Tel 56 88 31 76

LE LION D'OR••
Arcins
Tel 56 58 96 79

L'ENVERS DU DECOR•
rue du Clocher
Saint-Emilion
Tel 57 74 48 31

FRANCIS GOULLEE••
rue Guadet
Saint-Emilion
Tel 57 24 70 49

Places of interest

AQUARIUM ET MUSEE
Arcachon
Tel 56 83 33 32

MUSEE DE LA VIE RURALE
Mazères
Roquetaillade
Tel 56 63 24 16

TOP *Fishing platforms at Lamarque, on the Gironde.*
ABOVE *The Château de Lussac, in the commune
of Lussac, one of the five so-called 'satellites'
entitled to use the name Saint-Emilion on their
labels, because of their proximity to the famous
town, and the similarity of the wines.*

Specialities of the region

COUSIN & COMPAGNIE
(independent wine shop)
place du Parlement
Bordeaux
Tel 56 01 20 23

L'INTENDANT
(wine)
2 allées de Tourny
Bordeaux
Tel 56 48 01 29

EPICERIE DE LA TUPINA
(south-western specialities)
6 rue Porte-de-la-Monnaie
Bordeaux
Tel 56 91 56 37

PHILIPPE REVELEAU
(oysters)
82 avenue des Arbousiers
Le Canon
Tel 56 60 93 85

BERNARD LAFON
Les Conserves Oubliées
(unusual vegetables and fruit; verjuice)
Domaine de Belloc, Sadirac
Tel 56 30 61 00

JEAN-CLAUDE HUGUET
(shrimps)
29 rue Victor Hugo, Pauillac
Tel 56 59 60 78

BONNAUD
(patisserie, *cannelés*)
260 boulevard Wilson
Bordeaux
Tel 56 81 45 06

CADIOT-BADIE
(sweets, chocolates)
26 allées de Tourny
Bordeaux
Tel 56 44 24 22

PAIN MAITRE
(organic sourdough bread)
25 rue Camille Sauvageau
Bordeaux
Tel 56 92 28 64

ANTONIN
(cheese)
6 rue Fondaudège, Bordeaux
Tel 56 81 61 74

JEAN D'ALOS
(cheese)
4 rue Montesquieu, Bordeaux
Tel 56 44 29 66

DANIELE BLANCHEZ
(macaroons)
9 rue Guadet, Saint-Emilion
Tel 57 24 72 33

LOPEZ
(walnut tart, patisserie)
18 rue Gambetta, Libourne
Tel 57 51 15 76

LA MAISON DU JAMBON
(grattons de Lormont, Pyrenean
mountain ham)
Beguey, Cadillac
Tel 56 62 95 67

BOUCHERIE MARTIN
(*grattons*)
3 place de la République, Cadillac
Tel 56 62 67 10

Markets

Arcachon: *Wednesday, Saturday*
Barsac: *Sunday*
Bazas: *Saturday*
Blaye: *Wednesday, Saturday*
Bordeaux: *Monday-Saturday*: cours Victor Hugo; place des Grands Hommes; place du Marché des Chartrons; *Thursday*: marché biologique, Saint-Pierre
Bourg: *Thursday, Sunday*
Cadillac: *Saturday*
Créon: *Wednesday*
La Teste: *every day*
Langoiran: *Thursday*
Langon: *Tuesday, Friday*
Léognan: *Saturday*
Lormont: *Saturday*
Lussac: *Thursday*
Pauillac: *Tuesday* (fish), *Saturday*
Podensac: *Tuesday, Friday*

Vineyard visiting

GENERAL INFORMATION
Conseils des Vins du Médoc
1 cours du XXX Juillet
Bordeaux
Tel 56 48 18 62

ORGANISED VINEYARD TOURS
From Bordeaux: Tel 56 44 28 41
From Pauillac: Tel 56 59 03 08

ECOMUSEE DU PAYSAN VIGNERON
EN LIBOURNAIS
Montagne
Saint-Emilion
Tel 57 51 01 75

CHATEAUX LAFITE (45 56 33 50), MARGAUX (56 88 70 28) and MOUTON-ROTHSCHILD (56 59 22 22) offer guided tours by prior arrangement; telephone for details.

CHATEAU DE LANDIRAS
(AC Graves)
Landiras
Tel 56 62 44 70 (by appointment only)

CHATEAU GUIRAUD
(premier cru classé)
Sauternes
Tel 56 76 61 01

CHATEAU LATOUR
(premier cru classé)
Saint-Lambert
Pauillac
Tel 56 59 00 51 (by appointment only)

CHATEAU PICHON-LONGUEVILLE
(grand cru classé)
Saint-Estèphe, Haut-Médoc
Tel 56 59 23 00 (by appointment only)

CHATEAU COS D'ESTOURNEL
(grand cru classé)
Saint-Julien-Beychevelle
Tel 56 59 23 00

CHATEAU SAINT-GEORGES
(AC Saint-Georges Saint-Emilion)
Montagne
Saint-Emilion
Tel 57 74 62 11 (by appointment only)

CHATEAU LOUDENNE
(cru bourgeois, AC Médoc)
Saint-Yzans-de-Médoc
Tel 56 09 05 03

CHATEAU SOCIANDO-MALLET
(cru bourgeois, AC Haut-Médoc)
Saint-Seurin-de-Cadourne
Tel 56 59 36 57

CHATEAU ROLLAND-MAILLET
(Saint-Emilion grand cru)
Saint-Emilion
Tel Château Le Bon Pasteur 57 51 10 94 (by appointment only)

GRAND ENCLOS DU CHATEAU DE CERONS, *(AC Cérons)*, Cérons
Tel 56 27 01 53 (by appointment only)

CHATEAU MAYNE-BLANC
(AC Lussac Saint-Emilion)
Lussac, Saint-Emilion
Tel 57 74 60 56

CHATEAU D'ARCHE
(2ème cru, Sauternes)
Sauternes
Tel 56 76 66 55

SPECIALIST SUPPLIERS IN ENGLAND

GOURMET BY POST
(dried wild mushrooms)
13 Hawthorn Road
Sutton, Surrey
Tel 081 395 2391

VIVIAN'S
(verjuice, goose fat)
2 Worple Way, Richmond, Surrey
Tel 081 940 3600

MORTIMER & BENNETT
(goose fat)
33 Turnham Green Terrace
London W4 1RG
Tel 081 995 4145

HARVEY NICHOLS
(goose fat, verjuice, wild mushrooms, salt cod, fresh foie gras)
Knightsbridge, London SW1
Tel 071 235 5000

HERITAGE FOODS
(pike, zander, elvers to order)
Lakeside
Bridgewater Road
Gurney
Near Bristol
Avon
Tel 0275 474707

THE OIL MERCHANT
(verjuice, walnut oil)
47 Ashchurch Road
London W12 9BU
Tel 081 740 1335

HEREFORD DUCK COMPANY
(duck, duck fat, smoked magret)
Trelough House, Wormbridge
Hereford HR2 9DH
Tel 0981 21767

AUTHOR'S ACKNOWLEDGMENTS

Literally hundreds of people have contributed to the writing of this book – the farmers, cooks, winemakers, museum curators and artisans of the Dordogne region, whose generosity and enthusiasm for life and food was a perpetual source of inspiration; my partner Grant Muter, who, as well as providing constant encouragement, drove many thousands of miles while we were researching the book, and cheerfully ate his way through the recipes which made it through to the final draft, and many more besides; my mother Rusty Jones, who gave expert help with the testing of the recipes; the team at Conran Octopus, led by Sarah Pearce, who skilfully guided me through the busy schedule; and Marie-Pierre Moine, whose practical help and advice was greatly appreciated. Also, Philippe Esclasse of Stena Sealink, who generously provided ferry tickets so that we could cross the Channel in style.

PHOTOGRAPHER'S ACKNOWLEDGMENTS

I would like to thank Vicky Jones and Grant Muter for having been so much fun to work with; Karen, Meg, Cara, Sarah, Charlotte and Roisin for their hard work and good humour; Megan Park, John and Mary Wallace, Duncan Larraz, Di Rice, Amanda Poole, Jessica Staddon and John Stewart, for their support; John and Irene Hagemann for their kindness and Olivia Callea and Dorothy Dohm for their encouragement. My thanks go to all those people in 'the Dordogne' who were so generous with their time; their helpfulness and kindess added so much to the pleasure of being in the region.

PUBLISHER'S ACKNOWLEDGMENTS

Recipe photography (pages **30, 32, 35–6, 38–9, 57–8, 59–60, 63, 65–7, 86, 89, 91, 93, 95, 111, 113, 117, 118–9, 137, 139**)

Home Economist   Meg Jansz
Assistant   Cara Hobday
Stylist   Róisín Nield

Index   Karin Woodruff